Those Who Wait On GOD

Written By
Tony Hinton & Nicole Hinton

All scriptural quotations are from the
King James Version of the Holy Bible

Those Who Wait On God
Published by:
Tony Hinton and Nicole Hinton

Book Production by:
Tony Hinton and Nicole Hinton

Printed in the United States of America

Contents

Introduction 1

1. A Young Woman's Journey 2

2. A Young Man's Journey 9

3. The Chat line 17

4. Plain Foolish..23

5. Vicious Cycles 27

6. A Dark Morning..34

7. A Turn for the Better or for the Worse 41

8. Get Me Out Of This 43

9. Distractions 50

10. My Strength is fading fast.................................56

11. Here We Go Again...59

12. A New Chapter..62

13. The Counterfeit 74

14. Blown 81

15. A Word From The Lord 85

16. You Don't Date?..89

17. Breaking The Soul Tie 92

18. What God Has For You.......................................98

19. I'm Not Interested 101

20. Sunday Morning..103

21. Lord Is This You? 111

22. I Don't Understand 123

23. Wedding Preparation.......................................128

24. The Day Has Finally Come..................................138

Word Of Encouragement From The Authors..... 141

Conclusion 146

Acknowledgments 147

Introduction

For everything there is a Season, a Time and a Purpose...

Waiting on God can feel like forever, but in every season there is a lesson to be learned. God may show us a glimpse of where He is taking us, but we never know what the process will be in getting there. So we must be patient and most importantly believe we will receive what we ask in His name and in His will.

Many are hurting because they prayed and believed God for someone or something and it did not happen, or it has not happened yet. Some did not consult God for His perfect will for their lives. Maybe you prayed, but did not wait for an answer.

We have experienced this and out of our experiences we are writing this book. We pray that you will be encouraged and that you would hold on through the hurt. We pray that you will continue to press through the heartache. Go through the testing and the loneliness, because God is not only preparing you for someone, but for something great.

Those Who Wait On GOD
Chapter #1
Nicole

A Young Woman's Journey

My sister and I lost our mother when we were young. I believe I was ten years old and my sister was eight. My mother was a very loving person. I wish she could have been there throughout the time of my life when I struggled the most. However, I'm just grateful for the time God allowed her to be with us. Oftentimes, the memories of our mother are so clear that it feels like she was here only yesterday. The pictures I have of her helps to solidify those images in my mind. I remember her braiding our hair, popping gum and sipping on the Pepsi that she kept in a cup beside her bed. She would be popping that gum and tapping her feet while listening to her Michael Jackson records.

My mom always smiled, even when she spanked us. My mother would get up early on Saturday mornings to wash her car and to sweep the sidewalk. I remember having to come in the house, which we shared with my grandmother, as soon as the street lights came on and asking "How come we have to go in the house all early? It's the summertime, Fa'tima gets to stay out?" She would respond, "I'm not Fa'tima's mother, now get in here!"

Our lives changed drastically as my mother began to get noticeably sick. I knew God at this point; well at least I thought I did. My mother and my grandmother raised my sister and I in the church. They ensured that we were involved in everything possible at church. We sang in the choir, we were on the junior usher board, and we danced with the praise dancers. The list goes on and on. When my mom got sick, I didn't know how to take it. It was as if it all happened over night. My mother went from being active and full of laughter, to having a hospital bed in my grand-mother's room. It became nearly impossible for her to take care of us.

I believe she knew there wasn't much time left for her to be with us, so she made the decision for my sister and I to stay with my father. My sister was not happy about this. Our mom was sick and she did not want to leave her. I remem-ber being at the hospital the day my father told us to come with him. My mom passed away shortly after, and my life was completely altered. Life drastically changed when my sister and I moved in with my father. It was weird not hear-ing my mother's voice in the morning or hearing the crack-ling of bacon, smelling fresh coffee and seeing pancakes stacked up and ready to eat.

My grandmother watched my sister and I while my mother went to work, so we were used to seeing my grandmother every day. Now that we were living with my dad, we saw less and less of her. After my mom passed we went from seeing her every weekend to visiting maybe once a week. Not only that, we were no longer attending church. On Sundays my father would play Gospel music, most times he would listen to Daryl Coley and sing loudly around the house. My sister and I would get up eat our new favorite cereal and find something to do outside or in the house.

We didn't stay in one place very long so we transferred schools often. By the time we were in high school things were more stable. I remember attending my first day at Woodlawn High School, but I was not happy about having to walk home. Little did I know a simple walk from school would change my life. On the walk home, I noticed a girl walking in the same direction I was headed. I am a people person, so I asked her if she lived in the area. I figured there was no reason to walk in the same direction, on the same sidewalk and not speak. She introduced herself as Janice and as we talked I learned that she lived in a house right across the street from my apartment building. It then turned from an idle conversation about where we lived to a pointed discussion about God. First, Janice asked if I attended church, then she told me about holiness, being baptized in Jesus' name and receiving the Holy Ghost with the evidence of speaking in tongues.

I listened to what she was saying, but I said to myself, "I am already saved!" I knew who God was, but what Janice brought to my attention was that I did not have a personal relationship with Him. I believed, but demons believe also (James 2:19). She also began to explain that once I received the Holy Spirit, I would have power. This power would then give me the ability to walk right and to talk right. Now she wasn't saying that I didn't know how to walk or talk physically. What she was talking about was a supernatural change. I then said "Show me in the Bible where it says I have to speak in tongues to have this "power" and then I will believe."

I told my sister about the girl I met. I also told my dad that I met a friend and asked if my sister and I could go over to her house. It was a total set up by God; as mentioned before, she lived right across the street from me in a big beautiful house. Janice then introduced us to her mother. Her mom was an evangelist at the time; she sat us down and opened the Bible to the book of Acts 1:8. After she read it out loud, she then had my sister and I read what it said for ourselves. Janice's mother then explained to us that we

4

needed to be baptized in Jesus' name. Finally, they read Acts 8:12-17 and 19:5-6. I saw it in the Bible and I believed what it said.

Janice's mother picked my sister and I up early Sunday morning so that we could visit their church. Not long after we joined the church we were baptized in Jesus' name. We both received the Holy Spirit with the evidence of speaking in tongues a few weeks later. All this time I thought that you "caught it" and it made you dance, fall out and step on a couple people's feet, but that wasn't it at all. The Holy Spirit isn't like a cold. He is not something you catch. I felt like if I died I knew I would go to heaven. My father even came to church with us. My sister and I joined the choir. I joined the drama ministry and everything else I could put my hands to do, I did.

For the first time I realized this is what I was missing, a relationship with Christ. I grew up in church, but this was different. I now understood what it meant to serve God. The reason I wanted to go to heaven was no longer because I was scared to go to hell; now I really loved Jesus. I really wanted to know more of Him. Unfortunately, a couple months later my father came to us and said he didn't want my sister and I going to that church anymore. When I asked why all he said was, "I have my reasons Nicole." So there it was. We were no longer attending church and shortly thereafter, we moved… again.

I now found myself going down a different road than I was before. I started dating at 16; ever since I can remember I was in a relationship. I had little fake boyfriends before that age and I call them "fake" because I could not see them outside of school or talk to them over the phone. My father was strict! As I got older I experienced both long and short term relationships. Some of the relationships were verbally and mentally abusive. Some of them even got a little physical. In my first "real relationship" we were both virgins. We decided that we would wait until we got married to have sex. I remember conversations with my dad and he said wait until you're married or 18.

That made this guy a good fit. He was in agreement with what my father said to me. However, that relationship did not last long enough for marriage to be an option. When that relationship ended I started dating a different kind of guy. The guys I began to select seemed to go from bad to worse.

At 18 I started dating this guy who was a drug dealer. I had no idea at first, so imagine my surprise when I found crack cocaine under the seat of my car. I was young and I thought I was in love. I didn't think about how serious this was. I didn't realize that if I had been pulled over I could have gone to jail! I forgave him. In fact, I lost my virginity to him. I was 18 and decided I might as well get this over with. It wasn't because I loved him so much. I just figured he was not a virgin and I knew he would want to. The decision I made that night resulted in me being in the abortion clinic four months later and four months pregnant. Yes, I got pregnant the first time I ever had sex! I had no idea I was that far along. What I did know was that I would frequently catch him in lies. I'd even gone to his house to surprise him, but got a surprise of my own. There he was, leaning over the fence of his house talking to another girl.

There was no way I was having his baby. God wasn't on my mind and the fact that this was wrong wasn't on my mind either. I was not thinking that this was a life growing inside of me or that I would regret this for the rest of my life. It was a two day process that cost me $950 because of how far along I was. He said he was going to pay half, but the closer it got to the appointment, I knew he wasn't going to have it. It didn't matter because all I cared about was being free! I did not want to have this baby with him.

When my mom died she left my sister and I money that we received when we turned 18, so I simply went to the bank. I totally wiped everything out of my mind that would possibly make me feel like I shouldn't go through with it. His friend kept saying, "Man, ya'll can't do this. You should have this baby." He kept reminding him that this was our first child. My boyfriend never said he didn't want me to have the baby, but he didn't say he wanted me to either. To me, it didn't really matter because I knew the relationship wasn't going to last long.

I paid the extra money to be put to sleep. After the anesthesia wore off I noticed that I had no more headaches, no more sickness, no more funny smells and no more flutters in my tummy. As I lay in the recovery room I thought about my life and my relationship with my boyfriend. I thought, "How could I have gotten myself in this situation?" As I left the recovery room I looked in the waiting room and he was nowhere in sight. I knew he couldn't have left because he didn't drive and I had the keys to my car. I walked outside and there he was on the phone, talking and laughing.

I just didn't comprehend what could be so funny and how he could be so happy at this point. Why didn't he wait to walk me outside? It was the clinic's policy to not leave the premises if there was no designated driver in sight. I went straight to the car and got in. I didn't bring up my concerns. I did not want to get into it with him. I was tired! Tired physically and tired of the relationship, so with that being said I ended it some weeks after.

I felt so empty, but that didn't stop me from making the same poor decisions. It seemed as though abortions became my birth control. I didn't think about how it would affect my body in the future. At that time, I really could care less as long as I didn't have to have any attachment to someone I was no longer dating. I did not consider what the word of God says in Jeremiah 1:5. The word *conceive* means to form or devise a plan or idea in the mind. Before we were born, God had a plan for our lives. He knew how each of us would be conceived. It doesn't matter to God if we don't like the mother or the father. It doesn't matter to God if the child is a result of an affair. It doesn't matter to God if we were conceived by two parents who had a one night stand and were born out of wedlock.

It did not matter if I was four months along or three weeks pregnant. It did not matter if I felt that these pregnancies were a "mistake"! God's plan for our lives and the lives we carry inside of us does not change because of how they are conceived. He had a plan for the babies I carried. I had no one around me to tell me this; however I thank God for His grace and His mercy.

Years later, now out of school, I ran across Janice again and she told me about another church she was attending. I visited the church and loved it, but I wasn't planted. I had a completely different mindset from what I had in high school. I wasn't ready to surrender to God. I was comfortable with not attending church and doing "me". So I left there and was back to square one. At this point, I felt so far away from God that I really tried not to think about Him, but all the time He kept me in mind. Through it all I was still chosen.

Those Who Wait On GOD

Chapter #2

Tony

A Young Man's Journey

I grew up in church with my grandmother, Queen Esther Medley, and at that time neither of my parents were saved. The funny thing is I didn't know Queen Esther was in the bible until I got older. Back then I was young so I did not realize the seriousness of being a Christian. I remember seeing the church mothers lined across the altar kneeling on pillows, praying before the opening of Sunday morning service. There was a prayer line at the end of every service.

If someone was sick in their body the preacher would use anointing oil and pour it into the mouth of the person afflicted. I remember when my Uncle Earl first started his ministry. The services were held in the living room. My grandmother would still make sure that I was dressed up. I learned then that you could turn any place into an altar.

I was seventeen when my grandmother passed away and I stopped attending church. Not long after I graduated high school, one of my friends invited me to his church. I have been there ever since. In fact, he became one of my closest friends. Talk about divine connections! It wasn't until I sat under my current pastor that I gained a real relationship with God. Trust me, it wasn't as easy as it may seem.

There were a lot of trial and error situations that helped me to develop my relationship with Christ. At times I wondered how I was able to do some of the things I did while sitting under a pastor who taught the Word of God Sunday after Sunday. I was even in Bible Study on Friday nights. To be honest, I know exactly how I did those things: I heard what I wanted to hear and dismissed everything else. That's the danger of being hearers of the Word and not doers as outlined in James 1:22.

My story started with something that seemed pretty innocent. As a pre-teen I struggled with watching pornography and engaging in masturbation. I wasn't delivered until almost 15 years later. It was like a drug addiction because eventually watching it wasn't enough. One would think that there is no harm in watching someone else having sex, but when you entertain anything for a long period of time you will see it begin to manifest in your actions.

These pornographic images were stained in my memory bank and before I knew it, I was dealing with a serious lust spirit. Now at the age of 18, I was somewhat legal and could get into almost any club I wanted. What was my choice? Strip clubs! I knew better, but this was a new experience that I wanted to explore. My life seemed full of fun going to strip clubs every weekend and even in the middle of the work week. My friends and I would do nothing but sit around and waste time and money in these clubs. Today, I wish I would have never embarked upon that journey. I could have been so much further in Christ had I just obeyed the Word of God from the start.

Despite my struggles, I continued to go to church and periodically sing in the youth choir. Those times that I did not sing, more than likely I was doing something I had no business doing. It is one thing to be active in church and fight through your struggles, but it's another to deliberately live an unsaved lifestyle and work in the house of God like no one knows. God knows the motives of your heart.

10

I remember one Sunday some friends and I were sitting on the balcony at church. Our pastor made the altar call. He asked for the unsaved to come and backsliders to return to Christ. I turned to the friends I was sitting with and said "Y'all know we haven't been doing right, let's go down for prayer". They did not want to go. This event was so memorable because at the time I just had my hair corn rolled, and the middle of my braid did not come down to my neck which made it look like I had a bald spot. All I could think of was walking to the front of the church and everyone staring at that "bald spot". But, I didn't care, I felt such great conviction.

I braced myself and walked the "green mile"! When I got to the altar I was met by one of the elders that taught Holy Spirit class on Sunday mornings. I did not know much about it, nonetheless I know after she prayed, the tears flowed and my mouth started doing something strange. A language I was not familiar with – I was filled with the Holy Ghost! After I "came too" so to speak, I returned to my seat not really knowing or understanding the major change I just received. In fact, I returned to fighting the struggle that I was accustomed too.

I knew that a change had taken place because every time I did something that was not biblically correct, I felt worse than before. As a matter of fact, I began to appear bi-polar because one week I wanted to club and the next week I wanted to be saved. There was a war between my spirit and my flesh.

In my eyes, my life was so simple. I felt that I was not hurting anyone because I was just going to strip clubs and shopping malls to look at the females. Little did I know in the spirit realm I was setting myself up for warfare that I was not prepared to handle. During this time, I was still a virgin and had it in my mind to stay that way until I met my wife; but it didn't happen that way. Before I knew it, I had sex with only one girl and that was alright with me because I figured, "When I meet my wife, I will be able to tell her that I have only been with one female." Somehow I deceived myself into thinking that I would not go any further.

When I was 20 years old I moved out of my mother's house and rented my own townhouse. A year later I began my career as a police officer. Let me tell you, this did not help. For some reason I got a lot of attention from women when I was in uniform. To make matters worse, I could now get into almost any club for free and drink alcoholic beverages for free as well. It was on now! Before I knew it, I had already been with more than three girls. I even had an STD scare from a girl that was positive with a disease. I should have known something was wrong when she didn't want me to use protection. She kept saying, "I can't get pregnant, you don't have to use it". When I later found out she knew what she was doing, I saw black. I plotted to kill her. I pulled out one of my unmarked bullets for my gun, an old rug to put her body in, and I knew the tall bridge I intended on throwing her body off of - after it was done. That murder demon really tried to get me. I felt so betrayed that this girl would intentionally try to hurt me in that way. But, I learned a vital lesson from it. God doesn't give us commands without reason. He's really trying to protect us from foolishness like this.

Unfortunately, I did not learn that lesson until later. I thank God for touching my mind because I could have aborted my future for a moment of intense anger. God doubled my blessing because I tested negative. I took my Lord's blessings for granted because I still did whatever I wanted afterwards. How many times do we go back to the very thing God delivered us from as if we have nine lives? Paul said it best, "shall we continue in sin, that grace may abound (Romans 6:1)?"

I hear young people say, "I want my own testimony, I want to learn for myself..." Well, young person you hear many of the older generation saying how God spared them, but you may not be so lucky. The bullet may actually kill you or AIDS may accompany that pregnancy out of wedlock. So, take heed the testimonies of others. It may be your only warning! Nonetheless, the foolishness continued. I remember leaving straight from the hotel with a girl and coming to church. Don't worry; I sat in the balcony with everybody else that was at the club the night before.

My homeboy went away to college up in the mountains of Western Maryland. I never intended on attending college, but I gained an interest now that my best friend was going; so I registered as well but at another school. During his first year I traveled up the mountains almost every weekend. I loved the feeling of being away and having the opportunity to experience "the college life". The parties were epic and the fact that there were more girls to choose from made it even better. I was at his school so much that some students thought I attended.

By his third year at school, I was no longer hanging out at the college as much as I used to. The reason for this was Natasha, a girl back home who later became my main "Shorty". She may have been my main chick, but we were both doing our own thing. I was just having fun, so I thought. Before I knew it, Natasha was pregnant. Natasha and I were not in a relationship. We were both seeing other people. I knew there was a possibility I could be the father, but she told me from the beginning that I wasn't.

I could have walked away free and clear at that moment, but I started listening to other people who said, "Wait and get a blood test first! What if years later, after you've moved on with your life, you discover that this child really is yours?" Even though she told me I wasn't the father, I knew the only sure way to know was to have a paternity test done; I figured it was safe to take their advice. If it turned out I was the father of this child, I would have felt guilty if I had nothing to do with the child's prenatal care. Despite my own foolishness, I still had a good heart and wanted to do the right thing. Therefore, I stuck around to make sure Natasha made it to her appointments.

Natasha really didn't see any point of me going. She truly believed I was not the father. Despite her feelings and her giving me a rough time, I continued to be there for the remainder of the pregnancy. When she went into labor, I remember going to the hospital and having butterflies in my stomach. It was a girl, she was beautiful and tiny. All I could do was smile.

That day I remember thinking, "This long process of uncertainty and tension between Natasha and I is almost over." But the process was far from being over. Natasha and I still did not get along no matter how much I tried. But somewhere around the baby's second month it seemed as if things were getting better. Natasha began to talk to me more and we became more cordial. Now thinking back on this, cordiality probably was not the best thing. We started dating prior to getting the baby's blood test. By the time we did get the blood test the baby was almost three months old.

I remember getting the test results in the mail saying that I was not the father. I was really heartbroken because the family I thought I gained was now void. Crazy as it seems I wanted to father this child regardless. I continued calling her my daughter and I began teaching her to call me "Daddy". This was my daughter and I was her father. Natasha and I went through a lot during this time. Though we were now in a relationship, it appeared that she had more feelings for me than I did for her, when in the beginning it was the other way around.

Internally, I did care for her but I became scared of commitment. As a matter of fact I had become more acquainted with a female friend by the name of India; so I decided that Natasha and I should not use the boyfriend/girlfriend title. Instead we were just "friends". I guess this was my way to have my cake and eat it too. To our surprise, Natasha and I found out that she was pregnant again when my daughter was only 6 months.

Both of us were rather upset, we were young. She was upset because she did not want to be pregnant again and I was upset because I wanted to do me. Not to mention, I started engaging with another woman. Now I felt stuck. My perspective about moving on changed when we went to the doctor and the ultrasound revealed that it was a boy.

Towards the end of Natasha's pregnancy I knew I had to provide some type of explanation to India. I liked her and desired to have a relationship with her, but Natasha was pregnant. One Sunday after church (yes, church – I was going faithfully although entangled in this foolishness) I remember sitting in India's car trying to explain myself to her. I felt that I owed her an explanation because we were dating too (on and off), but she didn't know I had a baby coming.

I told her that I never intended to hurt her, but I had to take care of my responsibilities. While I was in the car with her I saw Natasha... staring at me as she walked across the parking lot. At the time I didn't think anything of it. When I finished talking to India I went straight to Natasha's house. When I arrived I was greeted by all my clothes and shoes

15

thrown on the floor at the bottom of the steps. Man, I creat-ed such a mess. I admit I was out of control, but I figured this much out: Men should never take the feelings of fe-males for granted. The man that I have become today is much different than the boy this story depicts. It's a little difficult even fathoming the thought that I caused this much hurt in the lives of these women. Yet, the truth is I did.

Once my son was born Natasha and I was back on track. We got along again and it felt pretty good, but deep down inside I thought I was stuck in this situation. "Boyfriend" and Girlfriend" just seemed to block me from experiencing the freedom that I wanted. So again, I insisted that Natasha and I should just be friends. The games! Consequently, when my son turned five months, the games I was playing back-fired on me.

Natasha began dating another guy. What?! She was trip-ping! Yeah, I know what you are thinking. I should not have said that we were just friends. I should have proudly accepted the titles "boyfriend" and "girlfriend". Well, you're right, but my young mind thought she should have just been my "main girl" while I had fun on the side. I know that's crazy, but the craziest part is that I really thought she was doing this to get my attention. She wasn't, she was aiming for her own happiness. Although I had my own house I spent most of my time with Natasha and the kids at her house. Now with her having a boyfriend this was soon to change. There would be a man in her life, but it wouldn't be me and I wasn't having it!

Those Who Wait On GOD

Chapter # 3

Nicole

The Chat line

Time passed. I started staying at my Aunt's house and my cousin introduced me to a new vice – chat lines. I called, left my description and spent lots of time listening to the descriptions left by guys. If they sounded like someone I would be interested in, I would either leave them a message or exchange numbers with them. Looking back on it, I thank God for covering me from dangers seen and unseen and not allowing me to meet some guy that could have been a serial killer. I was meeting random guys from brief phone calls. Thankfully, the guys on the chat line were not the only people chatting. As far as I thought I was from God, He was still talking to me.

I remember one situation in particular. I was talking to this guy (from the chat line) and we decided to meet. The following morning I was on the phone getting directions to where I was to meet him and I heard all these guys in the background. As we talked he kept changing the destination. Finally, he asked if I could pick him up from the flea market and take him back to his place because he needed to pick up some things before we left out. I was so naive. I didn't think about the fact that all these guys were in the background, screaming and laughing. I said, "Okay." and proceeded to go to the meeting spot.

When I got to the flea market I called his cell, but was greeted by an operator informing me that, "The number you have reached has been disconnected." I looked at my cell phone to make sure I had the right number. Yes, it was the right number. There was absolutely no way I had the wrong number. I couldn't believe that his number was disconnected in a matter of minutes! I called the chat line to get his description again: tall and brown skin with shoulder length hair worn in single plats. I rode around looking and hoping that maybe I could spot him, but I didn't see him anywhere. Unwilling to wait any longer, I drove off. As I drove home I began to think about all the noise I heard in the background and if it was even wise to have met him at this random house. Just as I was considering all of this, my cell rang. It was him calling from the same exact number that was disconnected!

When I answered, he asked where I was. I told him what happened and that I was headed home. He asked why I left and then insisted that his phone was never disconnected. He said, "I've been getting calls left and right." He thought I was lying and I thought he was too! I said, "I called and there was no way I dialed the wrong number. You're programmed in my phone." He asked one of his boys, "Yo man wasn't my phone on the whole time?" His friend replied "Yes son." The entire situation was getting old to me so I simply told him, "O.K., but I am still on my way home and I am not turning around. Maybe you can meet me somewhere else." He declined, told me to have a nice life and hung up! I looked at the phone said "Okay then"!

Although I was a backslider, gifts come without repentance and the Lord still spoke to me. Isn't it amazing how God loves us? As I drove home from this situation it fell in my spirit that this guy planned to run a train on me (meaning to have group sex) with those guys in the background. The realization so shocked me that I audibly said, "Wow." Back then I wasn't in a place to praise God, but now I thank Him for protecting me when I wasn't thinking! He intervened even in my wrong! He kept things from happening; He didn't allow the enemy to do some things that he really wanted to do!

Unwilling to submit to God or even acknowledge His protection I went from one "situation" to another. Yet God kept chatting. A few weeks later, while walking to the beauty supply store, this guy drove up in a forest green Benz with black tinted windows. As he rolled down the windows, all I saw was straight white teeth and a shiny gold tooth. He asked me for my number and of course I gave it to him. From then on we spent time together, but we were never in a relationship. He would give me money and take me to really nice and expensive restaurants.

He would always say he couldn't have a lot of women around. That he needed a main chick, "a ride or die chick." I wondered if I was that kind of girl. Could I be the "ride or die" for this 6'3", light skinned man with wavy jet black hair and a shiny gold tooth? I would shortly find out the answer to that question. One day he said he was picking me up and that he wanted to spend the entire day with me, but we needed to make some stops. He always opened and closed my car door so I thought he was the perfect gentleman. That day I discovered that this perfect gentleman was also a lieutenant in the drug world.

The stops we made were to make sure his "boys" were doing their jobs and had his money right. When we got to the first stop, he took out a small clear case. It looked like a ring box, but smaller. He pulled the gold tooth out of his mouth, placed it in the box then turns to me and says, "Listen carefully. There is an extra gun under your seat. If anything pops off, use it." He then pulls a gun out of the glove box, tucks it in the front of his pants, pulls down his shirt, kisses my forehead and gets out. Now I am like, God what have I gotten myself into, dude ain't got no FRONT TOOTH!

Out of all that was going on that's all I was thinking about. Not that my life could possibly be in danger, not that this man is in some deep stuff and I needed to think about what was really going on. No, my first thought was about his tooth. Now I have no idea why he took the tooth out, maybe it was to intimidate his workers or something. I don't know, but I was sure glad he put it back in! I didn't say anything else to him about the situation when he returned to the car. He put his tooth back in and we drove off. He pulled out a roll of money and added what he had collected to it and said, "Now we can enjoy our day."

After going out to eat, he said that he wanted to show me his house. It was very nice. He had safes everywhere, but I didn't ask any questions. We watched movies all night until we fell asleep. I never had sex with him and he was doing all these things for me so I thought to myself, I guess now he is going to want to do something. It was the next morning and he was in the shower. For some reason I didn't feel like I should have sex with him. Not because it wasn't the right thing to do or that I was feeling any conviction; suddenly I heard a loud voice on the inside saying "DON'T DO IT!" I couldn't shake the feeling so as he was walking back to the bed I told him that I was not ready.

I thought that he would want to smack me or something but he said, "O.k. I respect that." He was such a gentleman about it and I appreciated that. For the rest of the day we simply laid there and ordered take out. He took me home and as I got out of the car, God started chatting again. It fell in my spirit, "Do not turn back, do not go again."

He dropped me off and he told me he'd see me later and I agreed. As I was walking towards the door I heard a voice say, "He has the virus." Now even though I was a backslider and doing my thing when I heard "the voice" I knew I needed to obey! When the young man called to ask me out I made an excuse every time.

Eventually, he just stopped calling. I never found out if what fell in my spirit was true, but I didn't want to find out either! I was not the ride or die chick that he wanted! Even in my disobedience, God still covered me time and time again!

With no one to hang out with now, the chat lines became routine and addictive. As a result, I met a guy who later became my boyfriend. Let's call him Rick. We remained together for years. We would stay at his family's house, my family's house, on their couch and even on their floors. It didn't matter as long as we were together. He occupied all of my time. When my relationship with Rick ended I was very hurt, but God had a plan. Janice and I started hanging out more since I was no longer in a relationship. She saw that I was really hurting and asked me if I wanted to go to church with her that Sunday and I did.

As soon as I walked in the church I began to cry. I was so overwhelmed. I hadn't been to church since I was 16 and my dad told me I couldn't go to the one we were attending. I joined that Sunday! I loved this church. I mean the pastors were young and vibrant and I felt that I was really ready to serve God! I was in the choir and I was an usher. I remember one night we had an evening service and this prophet called me up and asked me about a husband? I answered, "Not until God is ready for me to have one." The prophet said, "You hear that ladies? That's a good answer!" Nobody at the church really knew me and quite frankly, I was tired of relationships. At this point, I felt like I was truly ready to wait on God.

Those Who Wait On GOD

Chapter #4

Tony

Plain Foolish

Who said God won't talk to you in the midst of chaos? He does. I was clearly in the midst of a chaotic situation with Natasha and India. I was spending the night with Natasha and dating India and only God knows the other flings in between. Lust was the strong man. Don't think for one second that you are grown and in control of your body because you are not. It's a spirit! On top of that I was completely unwilling to let either of them go. I clearly remember hearing God tell me to let Natasha go or He would do it for me. He meant what He said! Who has God told you to let go of? LISTEN! Or, He will do it for you!

Natasha started seeing someone and told me that she didn't want me staying at her house anymore. In fact, she didn't want anything to do with me and rightfully so. But this was hard for me because I stayed with Natasha on and off since she was pregnant with my son. The funny thing is, at the time I was a police officer. I thought I was numb because my job required me to be so. You really couldn't tell me too much. I thought I was unbreakable, but when she put her foot down I felt myself beginning to break.

I began to see her go out on dates with this guy. I watched powerlessly as he picked her up for their dates. I was really heartbroken and angry. Or was it selfishness and jealousy? I was simple though, instead of going to my house to avoid seeing this I stayed to signify. She wanted me gone but I claimed territory, so I thought. I could no longer sleep in her room, but I claimed the basement; I wasn't going anywhere! But, what goes around comes around. I deserved it.

Things began to spiral out control. The cordiality Natasha and I once had was completely gone. She was at my throat again and I was no better. I looked for every reason to start an argument. I remember one day Natasha's boyfriend tried to pick her and my daughter up, but he had no car seat. I figured that this was my opportunity to pick a fight with Natasha and her boyfriend. It's tough to admit, but most of my actions were a result of being heartbroken over this thing. Heartbreak was something I was not willing to admit and resulted in extreme stress and pressure. Acting on that stress came with consequences: I ended up getting suspended from work. My badge and gun was taken and I had a hard time sleeping and eating. But, it was my fault entirely because I was holding on to something God told me to let go of.

The thing is, during this time I was still going to church faithfully. Let me tell you how crazy I really was; I was determined to get Natasha back. One Sunday I was sitting in church and that particular day my Bishop was out of town. Normally, when my pastor was out of town I didn't come to church primarily because I was a babe in Christ, but on this occasion I was so desperate for a Word that I came anyway. This is the crazy part: in my mind the "Word" I desperately "needed" from God should have helped me decide between two women.

Thinking back, I was just plain foolish. Back then my relationship with God wasn't right so I should have known He would not bless me with a companion. But, nonetheless, I sought the "Word" that would help me choose between these two women. It's just laughable. The preacher spoke on the subject "Stay on Track". Mind you, I was far off track and not completely living for the Lord. The message should have impressed in me how important it was to get my relationship with God right, before I pursued a relationship with a woman. That should have been the result, but it wasn't.

After the church service I was under the impression that I should work on the relationship that just ended with Natasha, despite the fact she wanted nothing to do with me. Immediately after the service I told India that we could not further our friendship due to my intent to work it out with my ex. Sad to say, I completely destroyed that friendship attempting to save a relationship that God never ordained in the first place.

For some strange reason I thought the love I had with Natasha was real love. But let's do some math. Sex plus sex equals lust! Lust plus sex equals a soul tie. A soul tie plus sex equals emotional confusion which makes us think we love the person. I thought I really loved Natasha, but I later came to realize that "love" had little to do with it. Even that realization did not stop me. I was determined to make something happen that was not meant to be. I was stubborn! Needless to say the relationship I tried to save with Natasha never worked because the Lord ended it for me.

It's funny how our own sin will push us to pray when things don't go the way we want them to. The Lord was gracious enough to give me an answer. But it wasn't the answer that I was looking for. His answer is one I will gladly share with you. Your life has to be on track if you want something from God. Mine was not, which was the first mistake. How many of you reading this right now go to church faithfully, but live the life you want to live? God is not pleased with that and He will allow things to cause you to surrender. He will also hold some things until your life is right. Stop asking Him, He heard you; at this point you know what to do. You don't need another word, another prophecy or encouraging phone call. All you need now is a sincere, repented heart and a press for God that would forsake all else. If I could give my advice to someone I would tell them to listen to the voice of God.

One way to gauge if God is soon to send your spouse is to evaluate your relationship with Him and your relationship with yourself. Are you praying, fasting, and studying the Word of God? Are you living a consecrated life and abstaining from sex? Believe it or not, when He sends your spouse you will have to pray and fast for them. You will need to know the Word of God to help keep the devil off his or her back. You will need to be a consistent steward over your finances. You may even need to abstain from sex if your spouse becomes ill and cannot have sex for an extended period of time. That's real talk. Practicing these principles as a single person will give you the ability to properly face challenges in marriage; as well as discipline you in other areas.

Those Who Wait On GOD

Chapter #5

Nicole

Vicious Cycles

One night I had a dream about my ex-boyfriend, Rick (the one I met on a chat line and dated on and off for years). In the dream he asked how I was doing. I said "Fine" and then I woke up. I thought it was weird that I would have a dream about him. After all, it had been a year since the relationship ended. Breaking up with him was what drove me back to God. I was now going to church and headed on the right path. I was really involved and pleased with the work God was doing in my life. Exactly two days later, he called. It played out just like my dream. I entertained this new attention and we began to talk. I figured that the call was harmless; talking to him led to hanging out as "just friends." We had a mutual interest with staying in shape, which led to working out together. The more time we spent together the more those old feelings resurfaced.

Even as a babe in Christ I could have foreseen the pitfall before me. My relationship with Rick was always dysfunctional at best. Over and over again we would split and then find ourselves back together, but this time we've been apart for an entire year. I didn't know that the back and forth with Rick was a result of a soul tie. I should not have entertained anything further than the call, not because he was a horrible person, but because God wanted to continue the work He started in me. Instead, I chose to apply my reasoning. I figured I was doing so well with my relationship with

God that He chose to send Rick back to me. Still very much a babe in Christ, I had no idea about spiritual gifts. I was just beginning to understand how God would deal with me personally. Retrospectively, I realize that the dream I had about Rick was God's way of warning me. I didn't know at the time that I was to pray and wait on God to give me clarity. I later realized that God was showing me one of the plots of the enemy to take me off course; now unaware of God's warning, I felt myself slowly drifting backwards.

It started off nobly. I wanted to stay on the right track so I invited him to attend church with me and he agreed. I was so excited! I was hoping that he would give his life to the Lord so that we could grow together. Saturday morning Rick and I hit the stores to purchase church attire. That night, he stayed on the couch at my aunt's house so that we could go to church together in the morning. However, Sunday morning was a totally different story. Suddenly he didn't like the clothes he bought just the day before. I explained to him that church wasn't about the clothes. In response to my insistence, he assured me he would go, but he just wanted to wait until he could afford to buy something he really liked. Therefore, instead of going, he stayed at my aunt's house and waited for me to get back.

Looking back I should have said to him, "O.k. you should go home." I should have realized then that it was not going to work out because he had no interest in going to church. Instead, I told him I would see him when I got back and I was sad that he wasn't going. Again he repeated, "I will go when I have something better to wear." With that being said, I just left it alone. I got in my car and headed to church. I had a feeling in my gut that this was the time to make a choice, but I felt so weak! When I arrived at church I made a bee-line to the altar. Kneeling there before service, I began to pray and cry. I prayed that someone would say something to me; that someone would discern and pick up this back and forth in my mind. I was not crying out to God because He was good, but because I was about to break. I prayed that Rick would call me at some point during the service and tell me that he left my aunt's house. I knew that if he was still there I was not going to have the strength to tell him to leave. I began to cry because I knew I was going to give in to what was familiar. I was going to backslide and I knew it. I cried because I knew the possibility of me coming back to church after that day was very slim. I was literally at the altar crying out for help simply because I was not strong enough to walk away from him! I didn't have the strength to call him on my own and ask him to leave although I could have.

That Sunday I had to serve as an usher. I couldn't even keep my mind on the service. I was smiling and seating people, however in the back of my mind I was thinking, "God here we go again! As soon as I get free something pulls me back!" Then in the next moment I would think, "I am going to stay with you God. It will be o.k. I can do this!" This back and forth continued throughout the service. I left thinking I was fine, but knowing I definitely was not. When I arrived at my aunt's house, he was not gone. In fact he asked if I wanted to go over his Aunt's house. He was staying there and wanted me to go with him so we could spend some time together. I told him I would go, but not before I lay down some ground rules. I explained to him that I was now saved and I was not having sex until I was married.

He smiled saying, "Okay, I can respect that. You really have changed." His statement had me thinking I was truly doing something special! The enemy and the flesh will make it seem as though you have everything under control right when chaos is about to ensue. There is no such thing as "I will only go this far" because the flesh is never satisfied. There is no telling how far you will go or what you will do to satisfy it. I based his reaction to me telling him that I wasn't the same person as confirmation that I could handle this. I mean I was a changed person! I was being too hard on myself, right? I was just visiting him where he lived! I thought to myself, I am not committing an act of sin by just visiting. When you have to convince yourself that what you are doing is o.k., then most times it's not o.k. I was setting myself up for a fall.

I not only started to skip church on Sundays, the day after I visited him, but I began to slowly gather my clothes from my aunt's house. I tried to get my things piece by piece so it wouldn't be clear to her that I had lost control. I wasn't fooling anyone but myself! While I would be gathering my clothes my aunt would ask, "When are you coming back to church Nicole?" The only response I could manage to get out was, "I will be back soon." I rolled my eyes as I answered her. I couldn't wait to get out of there! I began to dread going to her house. I didn't want to be asked when I was coming back to church. I mean, I just wanted to be left alone to do what I wanted to do! I felt as though I was grown and didn't have to answer to anybody. I thought to myself...yes I missed a couple Sundays, stop hounding me! Actually, she only asked once and left it alone, but when you are comfortable in your sin you don't want to hear correction or anything that points you back to God.

I was now staying with Rick. I held on as long as I could. He started out sleeping on the floor, but somehow he ended up beside me...in bed. Well, you know how he ended up there! My aunt eventually stopped asking me when I was coming back to church when I went to pick up my things. That didn't stop me from feeling convicted. It was like I could hear her asking even though her mouth never moved! I no longer wanted to go to the house anymore. One day I decided to just pack everything and take it to his aunt's house since I was now living there anyway. That Sunday on the altar I'd asked God to send someone to talk to me. He answered that prayer, but in a different way. Church leaders started to call to ask about my well-being. I just felt at this point there was no need to lie. When they would call and ask when I was coming back to church I would tell them plain and simple, "I do not know." At the time Rick was all I was concerned about, but as the weeks went on our relationship began to unravel. As time went on it seemed as though we just weren't seeing "eye to eye". I didn't realize then that God wasn't going to allow me to be comfortable until I fully surrendered to Him.

We went through so much! There were times that the police had to be called and we were having arguments almost daily. Not to mention the abortions and a miscarriage. It was just too much for the both of us! These were some of the reasons we broke it off the first time. We still continued to go in this vicious cycle! We would break up just to make up! It would be months before we'd get back together and promise ourselves and each other that we would do better. Rick would say we didn't have to argue, that our love was strong enough to make the relationship last. No matter how much we tried, we just didn't get along. Once again the relationship ended and this time I felt it was for good. Here I was broken and hurt... all over again, but instead of running back to the church I just stayed away.

I felt so stupid. I didn't even have it in me to run to God this time. I accepted that my relationship with Rick was over. Instead of realizing that I needed God, I felt that all I needed was a new man. One I could get along with and he wasn't hard to find. It only took a 45 minute trip to a club in D.C. Kim, a good friend and I decided that we were tired of the Baltimore scene and would try something new. The club we found was filled with all types of people. Divided into multiple rooms, the club simultaneously played various types of music allowing people to move from room to room and have a completely different experience.

While in one of the rooms I noticed a guy standing by the bar. He was 6'2" and easy on the eyes. When I saw him, I didn't just think it; I said it to Kim, "He is going to be mine." "Get'em Cole," was Kim's response, and that's exactly what I did. I walked by him to make it appear as if I was looking for someone. When I knew he was watching I left the room and explored another one. I wasn't looking for anyone, I just wanted to be sure that he saw me and it worked just as I planned. I then went back into the room where Kim was. He eventually came over and asked if he could have my number. Kim said "Dang Cole! You said you was gonna get him!" I wasn't surprised at all. I knew exactly what I was doing. You see when you are very flirtatious you aren't just flirting, but you are being led by the spirit of lust.

This spirit is manipulating and controlling. It influences your moves and your motives. When you are in sin you think it is about how good you look, but actually it's about how bad the enemy wants to keep you in bondage! This "chance" meeting eventually evolved into a relationship. We went from talking on the phone, to hanging out in D.C. at his home or at his aunt's house. He was really nice and he had his head on straight. He was educated with a very nice job. I remember thinking to myself, this could be it. I could really see myself having a long term relationship with this dude. However, that thought wasn't based on the things I should be concerned about, like was he saved? Those things were so far from my mind, as I wasn't thinking about God, only myself at this time.

All I was thinking is he's tall, he has beautiful hair and if we did have kids they would be cute. I mean that's what my mind set was. Marriage wasn't even at the forefront of my mind because it had not been transformed yet; nonetheless, God had other plans. I remember like it was yesterday. We were at his aunt's house in D.C. At this point we were in a committed relationship. We were lying in bed looking at music videos when God spoke to me and said, "You are not someone's girlfriend, but someone's wife!"

Those Who Wait On GOD
Chapter #6
Tony
A Dark Morning

A few months later, when I finally came to my senses (so to speak), I realized that it would never work with Natasha. In fact, one indication of knowing Natasha was not my wife is that she did not want more children. If she did not want more children and I did, that in itself placed us in disagreement. "Can two walk together, except they be agreed? (Amos 3:3)" Sometimes we make things so spiritual when the answer is right in front of you. You are praying and asking God is this man my husband, but he is a Muslim. You are praying and asking God to relocate you to another state, but He already told you that your ministry is in the state you currently live in. Sometimes you don't need to wait on an answer from God. It's in plain sight. If it doesn't line up with God's word and His will for your life you can almost cancel it out right from the start.

After this revelation, I decided I would attempt to work it out with India instead. However, when I called to tell India that I wanted to resume where we left off, she informed me that she was now in another relationship and wanted to see where her new relationship would go. Yes, I know I was being extremely selfish and self-centered to think I could just call her and things would be just the way I left them. I was seriously tripping. I even called India's mom and apologized for hurting her daughter. That was the phone call that stopped me in my tracks. While her mother said she admired my courage for calling, she also revealed that she really believed her daughter met "the one".

This news was discouraging to say the least. As a result of my discouragement, I stopped coming to church and slipped deeper into sin. Back to the club life I went. When you are not grounded in God you will leave Him for foolishness you created and that is exactly what I did. I left Him and continued to do things that I thought I was big and bad enough to do. A few months later I heard the news that India was engaged to her boyfriend. I was even more distraught, all because of my foolishness.

I remember talking to one of my friends about India being engaged and he said, "Man, if you want India then fight for her!" Why did he say that? At this point I was tired of living in sin (again, it's funny how situations can push you into the arms of God). I decided to fight for what I wanted. I was going to fight, however, not for God or fresh anointing. No, I was going to fight for India . . . who was now engaged. I actually began to pray and truly believe God that India would be my wife instead of her now fiancé. I was as dumb as a sheep's fetus and if your situation echoes this one you are headed down the same road. If you think that was dumb, oh it gets better!

In January 2005, I officially began to turn my life around... all in the name of India. Not God! My "theme" prayer for India was "God! Please don't let me get hurt by this situation – if she is not the one let me know. I want your Will for my life, not mine!" So, I began to press toward God like never before. I continued praying and asking God if India was my wife to be. I was sincere in my prayer because I truly did want the Lord's Will for my life at this point, but I just thought His Will was for me to have India. Then something unexpected happened. I met another young lady and started to date her.

This young lady did not go to my church and in fact she was a really good catch. She was pretty, had money, a nice job and was a college graduate. Any man would have scooped this one, but I wasn't "any" man nor was I desperate. Nonetheless, I went forth with this new relationship. But things weren't right. We ended up sleeping together and this was after I turned my life back over to God. The conviction I felt was so strong, but guess what? We did it again. I was really upset this time. I even told her that if we fell again I would have to part ways. A few months later we slipped again, but I didn't have time for anymore slip ups during this period.

God showed me something that I wanted. In fact, that Sunday I went to church and while my bishop was preaching he said, "How are you waiting on God to bless you with a wife and you jumping from bed to bed?" Ouch! That was enough for me. I cut the relationship off and I continued to re-focus on what I thought God was showing me, India. I know by this point you're reading this and thinking, "This boy was all over the place." I really was. I was a babe in Christ trying to make my way through all the mess I had created. I was serious about pursuing the Lord's will, but I was determined to get her in the process. That sounds more like my will right?

To make matters worse, I had a reoccurring heart condition that was intensely painful to say the least. It felt like a brick rolling around in my chest which made it painful to breathe or even move. The doctors could not understand why the condition kept coming back. Test after test was conducted and still no answer. The cardiologist gave up on me, but God didn't. My doctor showed me an x-ray of my chest and the sack around my heart had swelled three times bigger than the actual size of my heart. The seriousness of this condition did not impact me until I saw on the news that a woman with the same issue died in the house with her son. But, the Lord kept me.

At this point, the Lord instructed me to leave the police force. In my mind I could not fathom the thought of leaving a career that I've spent five years doing. In fact, I said God if this is you allow me to get this job driving motor coach buses. At the time, I did not have a commercial driver's license or any experience that would qualify me to drive a bus. I thought I was tricking God. Not so! They hired and trained me. That wasn't enough for me. There was a pain in my side that had been plaguing me for some months, so I went to the doctor's office and they said I needed an ultra sound. The closest ultra sound appointment was six weeks away.

So, I prayed inwardly and said, "God if it is meant for me to leave the force then allow my doctor to take me off work for the next six weeks until this appointment." Guess what? I had a six week vacation. Who does this sound like in the bible? Yes, Gideon (Judges 6:36-40). Needless to say I left my career as a cop, a position of authority to drive a bus, a position to serve others. A humbling experience to say the least; I didn't care because God told me to do it. This move created a $12,000 pay decrease. I could no longer afford my town home and the new SUV that I just purchased.

I returned the truck back to the bank and started catching the bus again. My bus commute from my home to my new job was two and a half hours away. This was a drastic change in my life, in fact things got hard so quickly that I tried to return to the police department. They denied me because my supervisor lied on me. For years I thought this was the enemy, but never despise the tool God uses for your deliverance. I said, "God I know you did not bring me out here to die." No matter how much I cried, kicked or screamed He did not re-open that door.

One day I praying hard, just then the Holy Spirit said "You are not going back." I tried to worship over what I heard, nonetheless God spoke it. Despite this set back, India was still in focus and I continued believing God for her. During this particular time my pastor was teaching a series on faith. It seemed like the more I prayed about India, the more the Word would affirm my stance. When my pastor would preach, all I heard was "Hold on! The blessing is yours." or "If God promised it to you, it will come to pass." God didn't promise me India. He did promise me a wife, but her name was never disclosed.

This is why it is important for believers to take the Word as a whole and not the parts we want that would fit our situation. Had I taken the Word in the manner that I should have, I probably could have avoided a lot of heartache. But I didn't. I totally removed the parts of the sermon that spoke about, "Seek ye first the kingdom of God and all else will be added." I didn't want to hear that, I just wanted what I wanted. I continued to pray for the tangible and not for the anointing. So every Sunday I thought God was talking directly to me, and He was, but I wasn't listening to what He was saying. This nonsense went on for about a year and a half. I even began to tell India how I felt about her while she was engaged.

This was completely inappropriate. However, my "faith" was to the point where I believed that India would leave this man and be with me. It was never my desire to disrespect their relationship or to cause mischief, but I thought I was calling, claiming and speaking it into existence. I ignored so many signs. I even asked two elders that attended my church their opinion on the situation. They said it may not be that she is the one. It could be God telling you that there is another; or you may admire the traits you see in her that you would desire in a wife. Needless to say I wasn't trying to hear it. I wanted them to say she is your wife; we understand your position and keep believing.

Man, I could have been so much further in life had I put that faith elsewhere. Almost a year and a half had passed with me returning to God and believing that India would be my wife. With a sincere heart I really wanted God to tell me if she was not the one; so I could move on. At this point, I was tired and ready to give up on this belief. As India's wedding approached, I continued to pray. I was telling God that I did not want to be hurt by this situation and if He knew that she was not the one, please tell me. But, He already did. Yet again, I received another Word, "Don't let go!" The Word was on point, but it was for the individuals that absolutely knew that God had spoken to them. Oh, I thought I was in that bracket.

My confidence about this thing was on the rise. I was telling people that God was going to do it and that India was my wife. I had so much confidence in this thing that other people started believing it too. As I continued to hope, God would give me hints to save me some heartaches. One day in choir rehearsal, an elder told the choir that he felt in his spirit someone needed to let something go. At first I thought, "Is this for me?" However, I immediately erased it from my mind because I thought that the enemy was just trying to make me doubt. Truth of the matter is I should have lain before God until I got an answer in my spirit, but I just went off the preached word from Sunday morning. I was a babe, as I grew in God I realized that God speaks to you during the week too, if you give Him time.

It was now the week of India's wedding and I had no response from her. Then the day of her wedding approached, still no response. At this point I still had faith that someone would call and tell me that it didn't happen. Instead, I got a text saying, "They's married now!" I immediately became enraged and my anger was kindled towards God. I was so frustrated that my response to the text was, "I am done with church!" I was hurt! God how could you let this happen? This was a Saturday night. I went to sleep and that Sunday morning I had no plans on going to church, but ironically my alarm clock sounded and the song "What God has for me, it is for me" came on from the intro.

I looked at the ceiling in awe. I still didn't get it though. Believe it or not I foolishly thought this was God saying it was not over. How much delusion could one person possess; apparently a lot in my case. I was actually thinking a divorce was to come out of this thing. How dare I or anyone else wish the failure of a Godly covenant? Thinking back on it, I am disgusted with myself for entertaining such a thought. Furthermore, what God has for you is for you, it cannot be taken, uprooted or given to another. If it was, then it wasn't yours in the first place!

After a little while I just let the thought of ever having India go! But, in my heart I was still angry with God. Most people thought I was moping over India, but my real concern was how this faith thing worked. I was not upset because India got married, but the fact that I believed God so hard for something and it didn't happen. I remember saying while in prayer, "I had the faith Lord! What happened?" His reply was, "You did not want to hear Me Tony, that's what happened." Please make sure what you are believing God for is God directed because faith can only work in that instance. Even the highest faith in God cannot move His Will! Trust me, I tried it.

Those Who Wait On GOD
Chapter #7
Tony

A Turn for the Better or for the Worse

My unwavering commitment to God caused me to grow in Him. I was disheartened and disappointed, yet there was no turning back for me. However, I became afraid because I felt that my faith in God had diminished greatly. Moving forward, I was unsure of what I should or should not believe God for or if the Lord was even speaking to me. I still wanted to be in His will, but I didn't know how.

It's funny how God can use anything to get our attention. Imagine my surprise when I realized that He was using India and my stubbornness as a tool to point me back to Him. He will use the foolish things to confound the wise. (1 Corinthians 1:27). By this time I was so tied up in Jesus that I now wanted His will. Now when a female would take interest in me I would always say, "I am waiting on my wife". That was my favorite saying. Some of the ladies said they just wanted to be friends, but you and I both know what that meant. Eventually, I accepted that India was gone for good and decided to just press toward God like never before.

I was singing in the youth choir and adult choir. There was still a part of me that questioned where I went wrong because I knew God did not fail. Still not understanding, I continued attending church; learning how to master the concealment of pain, especially from appearing on my face when looking at India and her new husband. To stay out of trouble, I stayed busy. For the most part it worked. I graduated with my bachelor's degree, entered a master's degree program, fixed up my mother's old house, and managed to remain abstinent for almost three years. I was doing well in the Lord and was feeling good about my independence in God. But things slowly started to shift. As each project on the house was completed I had time to think.

Somehow I felt that the promises I once believed were coming, had vanished. The weight of that reality felt crushing. Before, when I believed God for India, I at least had an idea of what I was aiming for. I had in my mind how our life would be married with a family, now I was just lost. On top of having this internal dilemma, there were external issues I had to face. A year prior, I co-signed on a house for my mother, the house I just renovated. It was facing foreclosure because it did not sell in the time period we thought it would. I had to abandon my place to move into my mother's old house. I remember thinking to myself, "God what is happening?!"

Those Who Wait On GOD

Chapter #8

Nicole

Get Me Out Of This

I was in shock! I turned and looked at him as if he could hear the voice. Of course, he did not. I excused myself to go to the restroom. I looked in the mirror and begin to speak really low, so he wouldn't hear me in the other room and think I was crazy. I said, "God if you're speaking to me, then you are going to have to get me out of this because I want this man!" Yes! I said that! I mean I felt like this was the first guy who wasn't selling drugs, was nice, educated and fine! Oh yes! God was going to have to do it!

I knew God was speaking to me, but I also wanted what I wanted as well. I knew that the enemy wouldn't say anything like that, so it had to be God. A week later we were having issues and we broke up. Just like that! I mean it's like my world was turned upside down! The moment we ended the relationship I felt a change. Even though I had not returned to church I decided that it was time to fully commit my life to God and put my relationship with Him above all others! Not long after the break up, God began dealing with me about abstinence; so I made a vow that I would wait until I got married to have sex, but I needed His help. I couldn't remember the last time I was single or not dating. I always had someone to talk to or go out with, but I figured there was nothing too hard for God.

This time I felt compelled to obey Him. It wasn't solely about "not dating", but there were other areas of my life that needed correction as well. I really did have to grasp some of the things He was challenging me to give up. I realized that I couldn't participate or entertain the things I did before. There were also things I had to give up that I thought were fine. I did not see the effects they were having on my spiritual life. For example, at first I really didn't pay attention to what I would watch on television or listen to on the radio. If I liked it I watched it, if I loved the song I listened to it. I mean, I didn't think that had anything to do with my lack of commitment to God in the past or that it would affect my present relationship with him.

I felt like I was starting from scratch. When you have clogged your spirit with things that entertained your flesh for so long, you weaken your desire for spiritual things and I needed to get my spirit man strengthened. It had been a long time since I heard the word of God. I still hadn't gone to church yet, but I figured I would try listening to some gospel music first. It was cool, but there was one song I just could not enjoy. It was called "Yes" by Shekinah Glory. I would literally say, "Uuggh. I can't listen to this." I never knew what the song said because I would never give it a chance to play out! Now knowing the words, I also know the song has power. In fact, I cry when I consider what was really occurring in those moments. The enemy was trying so hard to keep me from giving God my yes!

The song asks, "Will your heart and soul say yes?!" There are some songs that are just sung and there are some songs that are written and sung under the anointing and inspired by the Holy Spirit. There are songs that will speak into your life and your situation and this was one of them. I wanted so badly to get back into position, but the enemy and my flesh were still working against me! The "dis-ease" I would experience was not just limited to a song. Each time I tried to attend church I would get extremely sick as soon as I got to the door. It was to the point that I had to turn around, get in my car, and leave! The enemy did not want me free! If I couldn't even listen to music talking about God or make it to church without feeling sick, then Satan was truly real and he was determined not to let me go!

When I came to that conclusion, I became determined to be free. The demonic forces fighting against me would have no choice but to let me go!!! I made it my business to go into the house of the Lord and to let that song play out the next time I heard it! I turned on the radio waiting for it to play all day and it didn't. The rest of the week I waited for that song to come on and could not catch it. Finally, it came on the radio Sunday morning as I made my way to church. I listened to the words of the song and I sat there balling my eyes out! Crying and repenting saying, "God all this time! Yes, Yes, Yesssssss! God you have my YES!" I got myself together almost an hour later! I went into the church and officially gave my life back to the Lord. It was now the year 2005.

Through this process I realized how much music influenced my spirit. I realized that just as gospel music had a positive influence, worldly music could also weaken my desire to listen to music that fed my spirit. I didn't think about the fact that listening to songs about having sex gave me a desire to have sex. This revelation caused me to decide there were certain types of music that I would no longer listen to. If I was going to abstain from having sex, I needed to remove anything that awakened those desires in me before the proper time. I had so many CDs that I would listen to and even play while I was sleep. Just imagine all those songs singing about sex and making love entering into my spirit. No wonder I had such a lustful spirit. The intention and purpose of music is to set a certain tone or mood! I had to change the mood that was being set in my life!

I thought about selling my CDs or giving them to a friend, but then thought to myself, "Why would I put them in bondage?!" So, I broke all my CDs! Now, you may think I was crazy for first paying money for them and then turn around and "waste money" by breaking them, but this was part of the reason I (Nicole) couldn't get my breakthrough. The music I listened to also played a role in keeping me in bondage for so long! These were songs I put on to set the mood sexually! These were songs that said it was o.k. to have pre-marital sex, that it was o.k. to have a dude on the side, and that it was cool if he left because I'd have another one to do it with all over again tomorrow. None of them sent a message about marriage or even monogamy! I had let God down too many times before and I realized that if I wanted different results this time it had to be by any means necessary, because I was not going back!

After making a vow to God, I got rid of my CDs and decided not to listen to any secular radio stations. I also made a conscious decision not to have sex until I got married. However, I was still dating and let me tell you that was a struggle for me! I would go out with guys knowing they weren't husband material. I mean it was just to have a good time and if something were to come out of it, then so be it. If they didn't go to church, we would work on that...later. I remember going to the movies with one guy that I had been dating for almost a month. As we watched the film he put his hand on my knee. I almost flipped out. I was like, "Look! I am being delivered from some things. I can't take no touch nowhere sir! Nope, not even on the knee!" After that date, I realized that dating was more tempting for me, especially since I was dating guys that weren't saved.

I reasoned within myself and said, "He doesn't have to be where I am. I mean we all have issues, he may cuss, drink and party a little bit, but no one is perfect. I figured that we could find our way together." I realized later, that was not going to work; it was like the blind leading the blind. Considering where God was taking me and what He was taking me from, I could not be attached to anything that would keep me captive or bound to my previous entanglement. It wasn't that I was better than anyone else; rather, I was on a different path. This path is called purpose and destiny!

Trusting HIM

I had now given God my "yes". I was now ready to surrender to God's perfect will for my life! If God said no, I would obey, but that decision did not come without a cost! In fact, it was a decision that was immediately tried. When God began to deal with me, I did not instantly cut off all of my male friends. In fact, there was one who I would "chill" with on a regular basis. I would go over his house and just hang out. This time before visiting I told him that I was headed in a "new direction". He said he respected that and wouldn't do anything to make me feel uncomfortable. One night I was over there a little too late and lived clear on the other side of town. He said I could stay the night and he would keep his hands to himself. He'd already proven himself, so I asked for a t-shirt and went to sleep.

I got up the next morning feeling good! I got in my car and said, "See, God. I was able to spend the night with someone I had been intimate with before and didn't do anything." Right then I felt something – conviction. What I needed to know was that it wasn't about him; I was still in this flesh also. The Holy Spirit began to speak to me. Clearly I heard God say, "I am not impressed with how well you stand up to temptation, but I want you to flee from it." "Yes, you may not have done anything, but what kind of example are you setting for him? Saved girls can lay with guys who aren't their husbands? What if someone saw you coming out his house?"

You are supposed to shun the very appearance of evil (1 Thessalonians 5:22)! At that moment I realized I put myself in a position to fall... again! This was the same story, but with a different person! How could I keep making the same choices?! After spending all that time telling him how I had changed and was no longer the same, I was in his bed with nothing on but a t-shirt and my panties! It was clear that this could not happen again and that I had more growing to do! One thing I was determined not to do this time was leave God for a man or because of a mistake I made! This time I was staying with God!

Later that evening, I got a text from him asking if I was coming over again. Right after saying I was not doing that again, I found myself struggling with whether or not to text back and say no. In some way it felt good just to be in the company of a man. Just a few hours ago I felt in control. I felt like I could say no and now I was going back and forth with myself. In that mental struggle I saw how my flesh turned against me and I was closer to falling than I realized. The Holy Spirit began to minister to me again and say, "If you know this is not your husband, why are you spending time with him at his house, in his room and in his bed?"

I got in my car and drove straight towards the beltway. He escalated from texting to calling . . . and calling. I didn't want to give myself a chance to change my mind, so I didn't answer until I was half way home. Safely out of range, I answered the phone and said, "I am sorry. I should not have stayed the night." He insisted that I did not do anything wrong and that he did not understand why I could no longer come over, but he didn't have to understand; I did. I told him I wouldn't be coming over and I especially would not be staying the night. Our relationship was one that had once involved sex and it was no point in putting myself into a compromising position. He made it clear church was not his thing and with that being said, we parted peacefully.

This situation convinced me of the seriousness of this walk. I was not in the place I was before or had ever been. I realized I had been in so many relationships, but what I needed was to be in a fully committed relationship with God! I needed to spend time with Him. I had no idea what He was preparing me for. I knew that I could only get it through spending time with Him; through prayer and reading His word. I had spent so much time with men and was always let down and most importantly, I was letting God down – my First Love. God wanted to heal and prepare me.

I thought that dating was going to prepare me, but it only occupied the time I could have been using to seek God. Time I could have used to ask Him to lead and reveal to me His purpose for my life. He needed to purge me of all past hurts, from broken relationships of all kinds; to teach me how to pray, to depend on Him, to have faith and to truly be faithful.

Those Who Wait On GOD
Chapter #9
Nicole

Distractions

Time went on and I was back in the house of God. Things were flowing well, and I was growing. I'd even taken on the role of armor bearer for my pastor's wife. One Sunday, the pastor of the church invited the members to attend a prophetic conference. I had arrived at a place in my relationship with God that I'd developed a real interest in spiritual gifts. I wanted to learn more about the various gifts God placed in His people as well as come to an understanding my own. For this reason, I was excited and definitely interested in attending this conference. My aunt and her husband were also attending; so I traveled with them and looked forward to whatever was to happen next.

It started off great. When we arrived I got settled in my hotel room and was pleasantly surprised. The person I was supposed to share a room with decided not to come. That meant I had the room all to myself. I read and prayed in that room every night after each service ended. One night I was in my room praying and I had a vision of one of the men (John) at the church. Now I didn't know him on a personal level, but he would give me clothes for my ex-boyfriend's little brother; I would bring him and his sister with me to church sometimes.

The vision disturbed me and I asked God, "Why am I having visions of this man?" I wasn't interested in him and had no reason to be thinking of him. I didn't think to pray and ask God for insight and wait on what He was saying. I didn't consider all the other ways God would warn me either. I just laid there and tried to get some sleep. The last day of the convention the hosting church held a dinner for us. As I was eating, John joined my table. I felt uncomfortable even making eye contact with him because he kept falling in my spirit the night before. Eventually, we returned to the hotel where I observed him talking to our Pastor. Suddenly, he broke from their conversation and asked if I could wake him up in the morning.

I thought this sudden need for me to wake him up was weird. On a normal basis, we'd hardly spoken two words to each other, so needless to say I was shocked. Nevertheless, I asked what time this needed to happen. He told me 5 a.m. Now I was a babe in Christ, but I wasn't dumb! I knew that knocking on a man's door at that time would not look right; therefore I asked if he had a phone in his room so I could give him a wakeup call.

He said his phone did not work. I was a bit bewildered, but I said, "O.K." Then John smiled the biggest smile ever saying, "Thank you!" I went up to my room very confused. I wanted to go back downstairs and say no, I am not doing it. I mean what if one of the saints saw me? I was so worried that I stayed up until it was time to wake him up. I just wanted to get this over with! At 4:56 am I got dressed and headed downstairs. To my surprise he and the Pastor were outside talking. I was thanking God in my mind that I did not have to knock on his door! I kept my distance from their conversation, but he still happened to catch a glimpse of me from where I stood. When he saw me, he thanked me for keeping my word. I replied, "You're welcome" and went back upstairs.

I was so glad that was over, but was still bothered in my spirit. What was that all about? Why did God show me his face? Why did he then ask me to wake him up? Instead of pondering the thoughts any further, I decided to get some sleep. Later that morning, my Pastor said he needed to talk with me. I had no idea what it could be about, but agreed. I was about to get into the car with my aunt and her husband when the Pastor called me over to him. He then went on to say, "There is a young man that is interested in you." Immediately I figured he must have been talking about a young man from the host church or a church we had previously visited, because in my mind there were none available or that I was interested in at our church.

I said, "O.K. What church does he attend?" He looked at me as though he was shocked by my question. He then said, "Ours, it's Deacon John!" The only reply I could muster was, "Uh really?" The conversation didn't end there. He also said that I may be receiving a call for a date . . . maybe out to lunch. I told him I didn't know about this because I was waiting on God for my husband. My pastor looked me and said, "I think this just might be it."

As soon as I got in the car with my aunt and her husband Brian, I told them about the conversation. They didn't think it was a good idea. Brian went as far as to say he saw me falling and my response to him was, "You have the wrong one. First of all I am not even attracted to him. Secondly, I am not going to fall. I have come too far to be messing up!" Brian wasn't having it. He said, "You say that now." I felt like he really had nothing to worry about because I had no intention on talking to him anyway. At least that's what I thought.

I was now home and not really thinking about all that had transpired. A couple days later I received a call and it was

John. I looked at the phone and thought to myself, the Pastor said he would call. I answered the phone and he said, "Hello Nicole." I said "Hellllo." He said he was calling because he had some things for my ex-boyfriend's little brother. I said, "O.K". I then asked, "Do you want to bring them to the church?" He then asked if we could meet somewhere else. We decided that he would bring them to my job, as his house was not far from where I worked. I have never been the type of person to beat around the bush so I just came out and asked him what the deal was.

I said, "Look, the Pastor told me to expect your call. What are your intentions and are you seeing the young lady at our church?" He was silent for a second and then he said my intentions were to call and ask about giving you clothes. I am not seeing the young lady at the church, we are just friends. I cut in and said well I see you both riding to church together and when they acknowledge you for things she cheers like she is more than a friend. He responded by saying, "The saints can't help each other out, cheer each other on and give a ride when needed?" I said, "O.K., well the pastor told me to expect a call from you. He then said, "I was calling to give you some things for the young man you bring with you to church." At this point I felt a little embarrassed. He began to ask questions as if he was trying to get to know me.

Then he asked me to come to his job one day, he had some information that he would like to share with me…so we set a date. After meeting up with him at his job he began to come pass my job just to say hello. I never had a man do that for me. He was a real gentleman. My co-workers thought it was so cute. I even started getting a little excited when he called. At first I thought this new found interest in John was because I hadn't been in the company of a male in a while. I made a vow to God and I planned on keeping it. I also wondered if this attraction I now had was due to the fact that I had never talked to someone who wanted to live for Christ just as I did.

I was always the one saying let's go to church and let's read the bible. However, this man would call, initiate prayer and share scriptures with me. That definitely won me over! I was falling for John. It just so happened that his job was looking for someone to fill a position. I was looking for another job and the hours were perfect. I needed more of God! At that time the hours I was working was 3pm to 11pm. I had weekends off, but I wanted to attend bible study and other services during the week; Sunday was not enough for me. I was going to receive less pay if I took the new job, but I figured that building my relationship with God was way more important than money.

I got the job and he and I began to talk more frequently. Then "talking" resulted in us courting. I mean he was different in ever since of the word, as far as what I was used to dealing with. Things started to get more serious, so we sought out to get pre-marital counseling from a mutual friend at our job. He also introduced me to his mother and some close friends. Things were really going well with us. I felt like I was in love. We were together every day since we were now working at the same job. He also began to pick me up and take me home. We would go to his home on the days he was off. We would just sit and talk... at first.

We had just returned from having a fun time with his friends and he decided we would crash at their house since it was so late. That was not a good idea, talking lead to kissing and kissing lead to fondling. At the time, I was not thinking about my position at church. It was not on my mind that I was a backslider and now I was living for the Lord. I was totally IN the moment. You think to yourself, we're not having sex, but the flesh ALWAYS wants more. You think you are in control, but you've really lost it! We laid there cuddling and talking until the wee hours of the morning.

You may believe that you have opened the door to pleasing your flesh just a little bit, but in reality you have bust the door wide open! We started kissing and fondling way more often and I began to feel convicted as I held a position at church as an amour bearer to the pastor's wife. I was a babe in Christ, but I still knew that what we were doing was wrong! I expressed my concerns to John regarding our in-appropriate behavior. I told him that we should probably go to our pastor and let him know what was occurring between the two of us. He then said to me that it was nobody's business; that it was between us and God. He made it clear that we needed to repent to God and God only.

I thought about it and I said to myself, o.k. I guess that makes sense. I then tried to justify the act by saying once again, it's not like we actually had sex. "Let us hear the conclusion of the whole matter: Fear God, and keep his commandments: for this is the whole duty of man. For God shall bring every work into judgment, with every secret thing, whether it be good, or whether it be evil." Ecclesiastes 12:13-14

Those Who Wait On GOD
Chapter #10
Tony

My Strength is fading fast

I was running full speed ahead in God. I was so expectant of this bright future, but year after year it got dimmer. First, it seemed like the "Christian" new year slogan was, "It's going get fixed in 2006, then expect rain from heaven in 2007 and 2008 is going be great"; yeah, yeah, yeah is how I felt when 2008 came around. I became so drained spiritually, mentally and emotionally that my body was coming to church and my spirit was staying home. Some of my friends called me as they were going out for a night on the town. Usually I say no but this particular night I said let's go. I had a ball that night! I didn't even have that many drinks and lap dances before I came to Christ and was living in sin!

That's how I know the enemy had a trap set. It didn't work though; when the alcohol wore off the weariness was still there. We can't seek help from the world because the help that the world can offer is a mere fake out to have you entangled in sin again or worse than you were before (Luke 11:2). I thank God for this experience because usually when I fell into sin, I would use it as an excuse to continue in the mess I was in. I knew God had a greater purpose, so I had to tarry some more. I didn't know what I was waiting for, but I believed God had great things in store for me. I don't know what you are waiting for right now, however God has great things coming for you as well!

If you feel that your strength is fading fast, just hold on! This is not the time to give up; in fact you are closer to your blessing than you think. Well, you may say that you've been waiting a long time, that this Christianity thing is just not working for you – do not measure the greatness of our God against your weakness in this current situation. If He did it before He will do it again! Think on the blessings you have in front of you now and when you realize things could be much worse your strength will quicken. I can relate, although I pulled myself together I was still in a weary state.

At this point I began to check out potential candidates who would make a good wife. Looking back in history, the enemy knew I had a surprise blessing coming because women came out the wood work. Not only that, but people who I love and trusted was telling me that I should check out that sister or date this young lady because I was single and had been waiting so long. They did it in love, but the enemy was trying to distract me from what God was doing. In some instances I did inquire about several of the young ladies, but God closed all the doors quickly. I even had a lady friend that I had a crush on in high school appear in my life, but I knew it was distraction. Needless to say I had to cut things off quickly.

We have to be very careful to depend on the discernment God gives us and not focus on the words of others. Sometimes people will pray and prophesy just to make you feel better, but you have to know God for yourself and when He is speaking to you. We have to be steadfast. Although I had no idea of where I was going or what I was waiting on, in my spirit I had a strong urge to wait.

God was teaching me to be content. This was not an easy process, but it was necessary. Wait even when everyone else appears to be getting blessed before you. I am a witness; you have a blessing that you will not even believe is yours when it comes to your front door.

Don't settle for second best by making a decision based on human logic; wait on the blessing that is gauged from divine intention. Though giving up may appear to be the best choice right now, hold on. What you are attempting to return to is designed to put you in a worse condition than before! Hold on! Jesus is the best thing that has ever happened to this universe and though many may not see it now, when He raptures His church many will wish they stayed in the race. So, stick it out, it gets better!

Those Who Wait On GOD

Chapter #11

Nicole

Here We Go Again

Not having an accountability partner kept me on the altar. Then on top of that, I kept having these dreams about John being unfaithful. I went from having the dreams here and there to almost every night. Needless to say, I was bothered! Being a babe in Christ, I didn't know what my gifts were. I didn't know then that God would reveal things to me in my dreams. I went to him and told him about the dreams and he assured me that they were just that… dreams. I was somewhat comforted by his words until I started to notice some tension while in church.

I was approached by a woman at our church. She asked if John and I were courting. He previously told me this would happen and when it did, say no because it was nobody's business. I felt horrible about lying. If God was in this then why did it have to be a secret? After that day, things became more and more uneasy. We were both uncomfortable and the fact that we kept coming close to falling wasn't helping either. Eventually we decided to just be friends. He stopped picking me up for work and it seemed as though he began to avoid me as well. After praying and asking God how I ended up in this situation, He showed me that h\He warned me.

I prayed, but I didn't seek God for an answer. I ignored what God told me to do and that was not to date at the time.

One sure way to identify a counterfeit is if he or she comes when it's bad timing. It is bad timing if God told you to wait. It is bad timing if you have just come out of a relationship. It is bad timing if you have no desire to abstain from sex. God is always preparing us and He doesn't have to do it in or through a relationship with a man or woman. All He needs is for us to spend some one-on-one time with Him.

After realizing all this, I knew for sure that he was not my husband. Unfortunately, that didn't stop my feelings from being hurt; nevertheless, I decided that I would never go through this again. I was going to be obedient to God and the next person I dated was going to be my husband. Although I was hurt, I was determined that no one was going to move me out of position! My pastor's wife told me that I should sit for a while, but I had already "sat" myself down. Being a babe in Christ, I didn't realize the importance of the position I held at the time, my gifts or who I really was! I was no longer going to keep the position as an armor bearer, not only because of our inappropriate conduct, but because I began to feel that God was shifting me.

All I knew is that I wanted to serve God and it was no turning back for me! This situation was not a good one, but it taught me a lot. One of which was to pray. I would sit in services praying and talking to God, and as time went on I no longer felt a connection to the church I was once so excited about attending. I wasn't a church hopper and I loved my pastors! I just felt like I needed more! I told myself I was not leaving and going back to sitting home on Sundays! I was going to stay planted until God told me what to do. In church one Sunday, I asked God to lead and guide me in where to go. That Sunday God refilled me with the Holy Spirit and He spoke to me clearly and said, "Go back to where you first received me!" I thought to myself, Lord I don't know if I want to go back there.

He continued to speak and said, "This is where I will set the foundation. This is where your husband will come and get you." It also fell in my spirit that I would only be there for a season and then He would move me. As God spoke to me I heard another voice. This voice I identified as my future pastor. It was a man's voice. However, the pastor of the church God was directing me to return to was a woman. When God finished speaking I said, "Okay God. I will hold on to your word. You have re-filled me and from this point on I have power. From now on I am going to seek you!" I just wanted more of God and I was determined that by any means necessary I was going to stay with Him!

Those Who Wait On GOD
Chapter #12
Nicole

A New Chapter

It was now the year 2007 and I was attending the church that I first received the Holy Spirit. I heard the Lord say clearly that it was only for a season and with that said, I felt in my spirit that this is where I would meet my husband and that he was coming to get me. I was so excited to be in a place where I knew the Lord was leading me to be! It was much different there! I was busy doing any and everything the Lord set my hands to do within the ministry. I was in the choir and would regularly attend Sunday school and Bible Study. I was a part of the woman's ministry and the singles ministry. The church was open for prayer every Friday night from 12am until 6am and I was there as well. I just wanted more of God. I had found a love that no one could replace. Every day I was consumed with wanting more of Jesus.

My lifestyle changed drastically. For instance, I would go to work, and if there was nothing going on at the church, I would go home, read the word of God or watch Christian television. I only wanted spiritual things in my spirit. I know what it took to bring me out and I wanted to keep moving forward in God. I had never been this serious about my relationship with God. I decided nothing was more important in that season than getting closer and loving on Him. I had been a back slider - sliding in and out, but this time I was here to stay. Therefore, I needed to stay in His presence. I would fast often for direction. Eventually, God began to show me things He had in store for me. I had hope! I now knew His voice because I spent time with Him. He began to use me on the job, in the market, in the mall…wherever I was! He was speaking to me and allowing me to encourage people. I wasn't afraid; I finally found my place in life… with Him!

Valentine's Day came and I witnessed people receiving cards with balloons, huge bears, walking and holding hands. Right before I was given the chance to start feeling sorry for myself saying, "God I don't even have anyone," He placed in my spirit how great it was to wait; that He had someone special for me. There was no need to feel down because of a day made by man; especially when He was going to bless me with someone to share not only a day, but my life with. There were nights I would feel loneliness settle in; right then this feeling would come over me. I would hear the spirit of the Lord say, "You're never alone." He was teaching me to be content! It was so wonderful! I would feel His presence and be lost in worship. During this time God was strengthening me, if I had not taken that time out with God, what happened next would have destroyed me.

It's like God had me hidden for a year and at this point I was totally content in my singleness. I was going to the movies and dinner by myself. I didn't have a problem at all spending time with myself. It was in this time that I realized what I liked, what I didn't like and what I was not willing to accept. During this time, one of my friends wanted to get together and hang out. She wasn't driving at the time, so I went to pick her up. As I was on the way to her house I decided to stop at a gas station near her house because I was really thirsty. I was pondering if I wanted to save $2.00 and just get something to drink when I got to her house or if I would pick up something from the gas station. I decided to go to the gas station to get a drink so that we could keep going- being as though the place we were headed was on the other side of town. It then fell in my spirit that I was going to meet someone there (at the gas station). As I was turning into the gas station I said out loud, "Oh Lord. Who am I going to meet?" Before I could open the door, a gentleman grabbed and held it for me as I went in. Immediately, I knew within my spirit that this is who I was going to meet. I grabbed a green tea and I got into the line. I was so nervous, especially when he came and stood right behind me in line! I paid for my drink and hurried out.

I didn't know why, but I just felt like running. As I was power walking to get back to my car, another man stopped me. He was lost and needed directions. I am terrible with directions and on top of that I saw the guy from inside the store walking towards us. When he got to where we were, I figured this is the perfect opportunity to re-direct his attention! You may be thinking while reading this why in the world is she acting so scary? When you want to stay delivered you get to the point where it is by any means necessary! I was not looking to date! I didn't want to be outside of God's will...again! So I said, "Can you please help him with directions?"

He began to help him; whew I thought I was clear. I made it to the car and I see him running! He knocked on my car window and asked me to roll it down. I spoke loudly through the glass, "I can't!" because I really couldn't. My car window was broken. So he asked me to crack the door. I did and he eventually asked for my number. Without much hesitation we exchanged information. Afterwards, I went to my friend's house and in my mind I am like, "I haven't dated. God you dealt with me about not dating and I have given him my number. What was the purpose of you telling me that I was going to meet someone?" You see God sends warning in all kinds of ways, but it is then our job to pray and ask God why a thing has happened or has been placed in our spirit.

I was still learning this. Without prayer I decided to give my mind some relief. I came to the conclusion that our meeting had to be for ministry. With that resolved, my friend and I went on with our night. As I was dropping her off I received a call and it was him...Jason. When Jason called, the Lord led me to speak on the subject of the Muslim faith. I did not know at the time that he was studying this religion. By the time we finished talking that night he shared with me that he knew it was meant for us to meet. He went on to share that he would always pray to Allah, but then seal the prayer saying, "in Jesus name". He said he couldn't help it.

So, he prayed and asked that "God" would send someone to him to confirm what he should believe and he felt I was the result of his prayer being answered. He began to come to the church I attended regularly and God began to change his life. We began to converse more as he joined the church. He even brought some family in with him to visit. God was restoring the things he thought he had lost and he felt that I was to be a part of this.

At this time I knew he lived with a young lady. However, he repeatedly said they were no longer involved and that she was about to move out as soon as she found a place. That was nice to know, but I was in no way interested in a relationship. I told him I was only there for him as a "spiritual help". He even expressed to me that he believed that God sent me not only to lead him to truth, but also to be his wife. With one breath I told him, "God didn't tell me that," but with the next breath I began to question myself. Why did I meet him in the first place? God could have sent any-one to be a witness. Why did I know that I was going to meet someone? When I saw him why did I immediately know that it was him I was to meet? I figured all that didn't matter because the fact that this young lady lived with him was unacceptable. As a man of God he shouldn't put himself in a position to fall. When I felt the leading to tell him this, he agreed. He said he didn't want to let God down and he wanted to be sure that I knew he was serious about his feelings towards me. I told him not to worry about me, that his salvation was more important. I was still unsure as to why this "meeting" occurred.

There was a shut in at our church and we were asked to write down what we wanted God to do and lay it on the altar. One of the things I wrote was for "Jason" to receive the Holy Ghost and he did. He also stayed there at the church and prayed throughout the night. Deciding that he was going to take a leap of faith, he asked his mom if he could stay with her until he found a new place. He was no longer going to wait for the young lady to move and she agreed. After this, we began to talk more often and it seemed as if we were closer, although during this time, we had not gone on one date. I began to believe that there was a possibility that Jason could be my husband. Why else would all this happen the way it did? I was faithful to God and I knew God. I had a relationship with Him. He wouldn't allow me to get this close and this not be "it"....right?

As Jason and I talked more we realized we had some things in common. We both had a desire to help those who were in need. We knew we wanted to make a difference. I thought to myself, "Wow he is a good guy and this is just perfect. Who knew that one turn into a gas station would bring this?" Jason had a son, so he asked if I would like to join them for lunch along with my nephew so they could get acquainted. While the kids were in the play area, Jason and I sat there looking into each other's eyes. In that moment and after all my running away, I finally gave in. "Okay, let down your guard." I said to myself. "He's in church and with you. You said you knew your husband was coming and maybe this is it." I was almost convinced, but not totally so I tried again.

This time I tried to block out the maybe's and said, "Okay, this is it." Just as the thought came to my mind, right there in the car, he proposed. He didn't have a ring, but I didn't care. If this was God it didn't matter. He later told his mom and she was cool with it. She was a little shocked; she said she never thought Jason would settle down so soon, but she supported her son. We never sat down to really plan the "wedding" and things were happening really fast. I didn't tell anyone at the church. I had just returned there and I didn't want to tell the pastor because I didn't think she would understand being as though we hadn't known each other long, but that was a mistake.

Regardless of how you think one may respond it is really important that you have accountability. When you are doing things God's way and you know it, you won't have any problem with telling your love ones or your Shepherd something as important as a decision to get married. I was not including God in my decision making either, although I didn't realize that. I simply didn't want anything to get in the way of MY plans, so I wasn't talking to anyone. I figured they just wouldn't understand.

Even though we just met, I always felt that it would happen quickly so the timing wasn't surprising to me at all. I said to myself, the time I waited and sacrificed was my time put in, but I never thought about the fact that he hadn't waited.

I figured well everyone makes mistakes, God isn't like man and He can deliver and mature you quickly, just as He had done with me... so I thought. I would soon realize that maturing me was a longer process than I expected.

We went to his aunt's house and she took a liking to me, but wanted to make sure that we were making the right decision. Her husband was an ordained minister. He was going to counsel and marry us; however his aunt asked us the majority of the questions. She asked us how did we know we were ready for marriage and my response was, "I felt like it was God." We were on one accord with what we wanted to accomplish in the future. It just felt like this was the time, our time. Then I shared with her the story of the gas station, how the Holy Spirit let me know I was going to meet someone and how things came to be after that. Jason really didn't know. He said he just felt like he knew I was it and that he was ready.

His aunt asked him questions about his last relationship: was he over it and really ready to move forward? Was he able to see her with someone else? She told him to make sure he was ready because "marriage is a serious thing." She then told us to go to her prayer room, pray together and then come back. I went ahead of him. When I went in the room, it fell in my spirit to pray as soon as Jason's feet hit the carpet in the room. I was to bind and rebuke every hindering spirit. Now we were supposed to pray in reference to the marriage, but I was obedient to God. When he came in that room God used me to call out personal things that I had no idea about. We cried together and I prayed for healing and complete deliverance first, then we prayed about the marriage and we thanked God for Him allowing us to meet.

Afterwards we sat and talked. He felt that if we hadn't met in time his life would have gone another way and maybe he would have lost it. He looked into my eyes and said. "God used you to save my life." I felt so humbled and I thought to myself, "Wow! This is really happening." Initially, we were going to have the wedding at his aunt's house. Her house was beautiful and we both agreed that we wanted to keep it really small and intimate, so it was perfect. As we planned, some individuals that were close to Jason began to voice their uncertainty about us getting married. They thought it was too soon and they knew that he was just in another relationship. My father wasn't too happy either. Well, he wasn't happy at all and decided that he wasn't going to walk me down the aisle either. That is when I started to raise a brow.

"I never pictured it like this," I told God. "I have been faithful to you and we are trying to do things the right way . . . at first." Jason worked at night and I would sometimes go with him to his job. It was becoming a struggle for the both of us because we were attracted to each other. We were trying our best to hold out for marriage.

Shortly after we began courting, my car stopped working, so he started taking me to work. When we first met he had a truck, but that belonged to the young lady he was previously dating. Now, he was driving a van, it was not in good condition so his mom allowed him to use her car sometimes. He would ask her if he could use her car to take me to work - a 30 to 45 minute drive. Because of the distance we figured it was more convenient for me to stay over his mom's house with him. Slowly, the things I said I wouldn't do I began to do. When we met I was very strict with rules because I didn't want to fall or destroy my witness, but I was now beginning to compromise. As I prayed I realized that I was not doing this God's way. I let Jason know that this was not how it was supposed to be and that I had to go back home. Things just got harder and harder and it seemed as though it was all starting to fall apart. Nevertheless, we set a date for November 25th, thinking that Thanksgiving would be a great opportunity for our families to meet.

I remember sitting at my job and going over my bills. I started considering how much money he and I had to make this wedding happen. As I sat at the computer I began to think out loud, "God what's happening? I don't even have the money in my budget for a dress." No sooner than I spoke it out of my mouth, Christy, one of the ladies at the job who I'd talked to about the wedding, stopped at my desk and said, "Nicole, do you have a dress yet?" I remember thinking, "Wow!" and replied, "No, I don't." She went on to tell me that she had her wedding dress in the trunk of her car and that it had just been cleaned. She said if I could fit it, I could use it. All she asked was that I have it cleaned before I gave it back. I called Jason immediately and told him. He was shocked! He simply could not believe it. He told his mom and she was shocked as well. Christy brought the dress upstairs, and I tried it on. It was beautiful and it fit me perfectly. The dress needed no alterations whatsoever. This moment made me feel better.

I began to think, "Okay, maybe this is going to work out after all." I never would have imagined not having a dress and not having to pay for it. I took pictures in the dress and sent them to Jason's mom. She thought it was beautiful as well. We were getting married, we were going to have a wedding and it was happening in that beautiful dress. It was all settled until Jason expressed to me that he was stressed out. He then told me that he would like to just get married at the court house. I was blown at this point. This was not looking like what I imagined, but I said nothing. I didn't want him to think that I was caught up in the glitz and glamorous part of a wedding; so instead I began to pray and ask God what this all meant. A short time later, Jason decided that we should apply for an apartment. His plan was that as soon as we were approved for the apartment, we would go to the courthouse and get married. This way we wouldn't move in together before we were married. I wasn't sure about this at all! My car was no longer working, we had no money saved and here we were – about to be married and at a court house. These were not the only issues. The more I prayed the more things began to arise. As I prayed, I kept hearing "suicide". I couldn't shake the thought and wondered who I knew was planning to take their life. Jason came to mind and one day it all became clear.

On that day my co-worker, Brad, took me to Jason's job to get his mother's house key. I was going to wait there until he got off. I felt funny while at Jason's job and noticed the he kept looking around a lot. When I got to his mom's house I called him. After a minute of being on the phone he said one of his clients needed to use the phone as he worked at a group home. He said that he'd call me right back. I agreed and we hung up. As soon as I hung up the phone, it fell in my spirit to call right back.

I thought to myself, and then said out loud, "Why? We just got off the phone." But I was obedient and dialed the number. His co-worker answered the phone – not a client. I asked to speak to Jason, but his co-worker said he left and would be back later. As he was speaking, the truck Jason used to drive (the one that belonged to his ex-girlfriend) came to mind, so I asked if he got in a specifically described truck and his co-worker said yes. I told him thank you and ended the call. I then saw a vision of them sitting not too far from the job. I then called Jason on his cell; it rang a few times then went to voicemail. I was so angry that I called his job back and asked his co-worker for the address and the number to a cab service. Without hesitation, he asked me to hold while he got it for me. The more I thought about him not answering his cell phone and on top of that the vision, the angrier I became!

I imagined myself going to the window and just swinging! Just then I heard a still small voice saying, "Remember who you are." I mean that kept ringing in my ear! It didn't matter what was going on! I was a woman of God and how would it look for me to be fighting in the street? I hung up the phone and I called Jason's cell again, but received no answer. I called again, but this time I hung up after the 3rd ring and I did so about four more times so that he would get the picture that I knew something was wrong. I began to cry, scream and ask "Why!" out loud. I mean I had tried my best to do things the right way. We did not date and I ran from temptation at times I wanted to give all the way in. This feeling was all too familiar. It was during this time that I had the opportunity to think and to PRAY. In a place of prayer I realized these things didn't start happening until I really started to ask God what HE thought about our relationship.

Then the Holy Spirit started to reveal even more. I began to realize that I did not seek God's will for my life which included, but was not limited to a spouse! Instead, I just came to the conclusion that this had to be it. We were assuming God was in it because of signs. For example, he was following me to church one evening for bible study and a car cut in front of him. He called me and said the tags on the car that was now behind me and in front of him said, "GODS WILL". We were going off things like that, but how you know and know for sure is to go to God FIRST and then WAIT on His answer - whatever it may be and however he chooses to reveal it! I was learning this the hard way! Even after talking to God and hearing the Holy Spirit speak to me, I was still confused. I still wanted a "sign" to see if Jason was "it" or not! While I was pondering all of this Jason called back, but I didn't answer.

I allowed him to call me like I was calling him. I was not answering the phone. I wanted him to know that I knew. He left work and came to his mother's house where I was. By the time he arrived I'd fallen asleep. He didn't have a key, so he threw rocks at the window to wake me so I could let him in. This seems cute doesn't it? No! I was still furious! He could tell from the look on my face that I was not happy and that I had been crying. I told him that I knew that he had been seeing "her" and I don't know why he felt the need to lie to me. He said he was sorry and that they met up because she mentioned not being able live without him. He then asked if I could talk with her, but I told him that would only worsen the situation considering the fact that I was the woman he was choosing to marry. Furthermore, what exactly was I supposed to say to her? He began to express that he wanted to marry me, but was worried about her. He then went on to say, "Honestly, I don't know how I'd feel now if I saw her with someone else." After sharing that with me, he then went on to say he felt that in time he would be able to get over it.

Those Who Wait On GOD
Chapter #13
Nicole
The Counterfeit

We were still moving forward with the wedding and the plan to rent an apartment. In preparation to fill out the application, I asked my supervisor to print out my pay stubs. While I waited for her to do so, I couldn't help but think about the direction that he and I were going in. Was I really ready to sign a lease, get married at the court house, have no honeymoon and just pray that we'd make it? As my supervisor was preparing my pay stubs, I sat there and began to pray. I said, "Lord, if it isn't for us to get this apartment I pray that you intervene in any way you see fit. I also asked that God would give me a sign. I asked that his phone would ring repeatedly. I just wanted a final answer. I no longer wanted to be confused or go any further if this was not God's will for him or me.

I said this time, "If you give me a sign I will listen! Please get me out of this if I am not in your will." It was then that I heard my phone vibrating. It was Jason. I asked him was he ready for me to come downstairs and his answer gave me chills! He told me that three bolts came off the tire of the van and that he would be a while picking me up. Consequently, we would not make it to the apartment. I sat there in disbelief. I knew what I had prayed and now I was in shock. This is not it?! He is not my husband?! Wait a minute God! I tried to remember if I said show me these things if he wasn't it or if the timing was wrong. Now I knew good and well what I asked! Isn't that something?! You ask for God to reveal certain things, but at the end of the day, you don't really want to know.

I will say this, if you ask God to remove any and everything out of your life that would hinder your walk with Him, you may find yourself in a season of isolation. When you ask to be in the perfect will of God expect for your entire life to take a turn! It may seem like it's for the worst at times but it's all working together. God strategically allows certain situations and will at times use the mess we made to catapult us into our destiny! You have to be ready when you give God your "yes" because He may not only change the partner you are dating, but your dream job, major in school, the area you live in and your surroundings as well!

After getting over the shock of my "answered prayer" I knew that I had to talk with Jason. I then told my supervisor that she didn't have to print out the stubs. I sat at my desk and waited for Jason to call. He said he would be awhile which meant I had a while to think. I kept going over my prayer in my mind. What did I ask specifically? I said, "Lord if it isn't for us to do this." I just asked God to please make it plain to me. One thing I did know was that we were not to get this apartment and the wedding could not take place . . . for now anyway. About a half hour later he called and said he was downstairs. As soon as I got in the van his phone began to ring repeatedly. It was impossible to deny – God was answering my prayers. I told him that we needed to talk and before I could get anything out he said, "Maybe now is not the time for marriage." I almost got angry!

I mean yes I was going to tell him, but I knew the reason I was saying it. I was curious as to why he was saying it and before I could get it out! Nevertheless I agreed. Although God made it plain that Jason was not my husband I still tried to continue the relationship. It seemed purposeless and it began to feel like we weren't even a couple. Other things began to manifest as well. He expressed that he would like for me to sign a pre-nuptial agreement when we did decide to get married because though he didn't have much now, he knew he would be wealthy. It didn't matter that he didn't have lots of money because I am not a materialistic girl, but I said to Jason, "You aren't wealthy now, so anything you obtain within the relationship we will be building together." Not that I have a problem with a pre-nuptial agreement for somebody else, but to me that is saying there is an option for divorce!

I just didn't see my future husband and I going through things like this. I began to feel like these little things were definitely a sign that he was not my husband. God doesn't always send someone that you will constantly be in agreement with nor is a person disqualified just because they do things differently than you. The problem was that this was not adding up with my prayers. God answered everyone and responded in a way in which I could understand. There are certain characteristics God showed me concerning my husband and this did not resemble them. Secondly, and most importantly, it was clear that he could not carry me spiritually. I was worn out and we just didn't see eye to eye. I didn't want him to sneak and do things because he knew that I wasn't comfortable with it. He needed to get to a place in God where he could grow and stand on his own. I did not want to be a "spiritual cougar".

A spiritual cougar is someone further along in the Lord dating or planning to marry a babe and God has NOT given them the go! This can be dangerous. When you are more mature and grounded in Christ there are certain things you may not do. You may have a greater conviction concerning some things because of the place you are in God. This walk is compared to a baby because a baby has to learn everything from scratch. They have to learn to crawl, and then learn to walk. This is the same with babes in Christ. Some are trying to make a person grow to the level they are on and it's a process. You have to be careful of who you are yoked with. Just because they are "in" the church doesn't mean that you two will be equally yoked. If God is preparing you for ministry, but this person you are "courting" hasn't gotten their run out, still wants to party and still wants to go in the places that God has called you out of. It will not only be a struggle, but you are also adding unnecessary warfare in your life.

This is why it is important to seek God in the beginning. It's harder to walk away when you have invested time in a person. You must also be careful of soul ties. Not all soul ties are bad, but it becomes dangerous when a person is a threat to your spiritual growth. It also becomes an issue when they are not headed in the same direction as you are or if they are only supposed to be with you for a season. It is clear you have a soul tie when you are no longer with the person, yet continue to think of them. Even if you are married or they are married and have gone on with their lives. Another indication that you have a soul tie is when God is separating you from a person and you struggle with it- even if they have treated you badly.

Soul ties aren't just sexual, as there are emotional soul ties as well; however remember that there is nothing too strong that you are not able to walk away from (read 1 Corinthians10:13)! All you need is a desire to serve God and to be in His will; even if that means leaving the man, woman, relationship or friendship.

I expressed my feelings to Jason. I told him that I didn't think we were on one accord with the marriage or our expectations of one another. I also shared with him that it fell in my spirit that God really wanted him to seek Him and to be stronger in the faith. I further advised that God wanted him to develop a relationship with Him before going any further with anyone else. After expressing to Jason that he needed to let God finish the work that He began in him, Jason felt defeated. He didn't believe the wedding was going to happen any time soon. He felt that if we waited for him to develop his relationship with God on his own then we would never get married, so his solution was, "Let's just get married." By then I knew he was not ready. After praying and holding off the wedding, things drastically changed between us.

Since my car broke down he'd consistently picked me up from work. Now, he would say he was going to pick me up, then arrive really late. One time he told me that he could not come and get me at the last minute and that I needed to find a ride. I asked, "How am I supposed to find a ride this late?" He hung up in my ear and would not answer the phone when I called back. I was so hurt. I remember looking at the phone and crying. I couldn't believe that he would do me like that. The man that just asked me to marry him was now treating me like I never meant anything to him. When God shows you what you asked, but you continue to entertain it and not cut it off when He says to, you put yourself in a position to go through unnecessary hurt. I couldn't even be angry at Jason.

Some of you are still harboring bitterness and hatred towards a man or woman who did you wrong and have yet to consider the part you played. You need to release it right now! Some of you are in another relationship or even married, still holding on to what the boyfriend or girlfriend

78

from five years ago did. Release it! No, what they did was not right, but God always sends warning to His children. Thank God for His grace and mercy! Thank God that you have happiness in Jesus and if you don't know how to have happiness in Jesus alone...keep reading!

A co-worker lived around the corner from me and I never knew it. She gave me a ride home that night and until I purchased a new car! After all we had gone through, even with the decision not to marry, he told me that he still wanted to be with me. Shortly after this conversation he let me know that for financial reasons he had to move back into his home, with his previous girlfriend. I was hurt, but I told him that I was okay with him going on with his plans. I was not going to continue a relationship with him living with someone else. I also told him to remember that God truly saved him and that He did not save him to return to bondage. I let him know that I would be praying for him and that he shouldn't stop coming to church and to consider bringing the young lady as well. I knew that it wasn't about me, but it was about what God wanted to do in and through his life!

After we ended the conversation I sat there staring at the dress I was supposed to wear in just a few weeks. Then I begin to think about what I would say to those who knew I was going to get married. I figured, hey... things happen and it was better to do the right thing now then go through with a wedding and end up divorced months or possibly weeks later! I went to work the next day and gave the dress back to Christy.

I was dreading all the questions, but I guess she decided to save me the trouble. I let my supervisor know that I no longer needed to take off the days I put in for. To my surprise my supervisor (Peggy) was relieved. She said God was going to send my Boaz and it would all fall into place like I always said God would allow it too.

Those Who Wait On GOD

Chapter #14

Nicole

Blown

It was now Sunday afternoon. Service had ended at church but I sat there thinking about all that had transpired and I began to cry. I couldn't believe that as soon as I said a little prayer the relationship was over! I thought to myself, what happened? Why did I go through this? What was all this for? "I am living right," I said to God. "I had my wedding dress, all of my family knew, and I had time set aside at my job for a honeymoon that was no longer going to take place." I began to think on how I told people I knew God was in the relationship and that he was my husband! I felt a little embarrassed, but instead of being stuck on that, I just prayed that God would give me strength.

No one at church knew what I was going through; as I sat there crying, the woman who tarried with Jason to receive the Holy Ghost came over and asked about him. She hadn't seen him in church so she was concerned. I couldn't get anything out; I just began to cry again. She comforted me and expressed that God showed her that he wanted to marry me. However, she strongly felt that if he was the husband God had for me then he would come back if it were the Lord's will. All I could think was, "What in the world is going on?" I wrestled with this, but I was determined I wasn't going to call him or try to contact him. I was not going to chase after any man and I was not going to be hurt again. So, I was torn...again.

I thought to myself, do I wait for Jason to come back or is there another? One thing I did know was that I was not dating and I was now going to seek God first. I was determined that I was not going to go through what I had just experienced. No way! Not ever! I thought back to when I heard God give me specific instructions and in the past I had listened to everyone else but Him. I began to realize that it wasn't about what anyone else thought. It didn't matter if someone thought that I was the perfect match for them or someone they knew. It didn't matter if a guy thought I was his wife because of the "anointing" on my life. I was going to listen to God and obey. I began to fast and read God's word more than ever. I decided that this time, I was going to pray when things fell in my spirit and I was not going to move unless I was clear God was speaking.

I kept going over the things that made me feel like Jason was the one. There was the dress…wasn't that a sign? Then there was the prayer and us not being able to go to the apartments. I then thought to myself, what about the fact that I knew I would meet someone and knowing it was him when I saw him? Was that a sign? These thoughts plagued me because I didn't want to meet someone new if I was supposed to be with Jason. However, I also didn't want to spend my life waiting on him and pass up the man that God truly intended for me to be with.

Settling my mind and my spirit was a job only God could do! I needed to know what to do so I prayed, God please make this plain. For almost a year after this I was still torn - waiting on a man who would probably never come. Praying that God would send him or at least allow me to see him if it was to be - still looking for a sign.

I was watching television and it fell in my spirit that the young lady that Jason was seeing was going to call me. To my surprise, she called towards the end of the week. She wanted to know when we met, how we met, and how it was that we were getting married so fast. She said she saw the picture of me in my dress. She wondered how was it that he had been with her for years, but in a matter of months he was about to marry me. It fell in my spirit that she was asking these questions because she wanted to make sure that Jason didn't cheat on her. I answered her questions and I told her that I thought he was my husband. I told her that I would not contact him out of respect for her and that she had nothing to worry about, on my end.

I knew from the call that they were getting back together and that he allowed her to question me about whatever she wanted so they could go forth in their relationship. I got off the phone feeling angry and hurt! It felt like I meant nothing to him. That call was confirmation to me that Jason wasn't my husband, but I still had the thought in the back of my mind. Sometimes we look for some deep revelation when it's right in front of our face. The more I prayed the more dreams God would give me and by now I was convinced that maybe I should not be waiting for his return. The woman (Evangelist Booker who had tarried with Jason) and I became very close. I looked to her for spiritual guidance. She really encouraged me during the wait.

One day God began to use her prophetically and she said you won't be here (meaning our church) much longer. She said God is going to do great things through you. She said hold on. She also brought up a woman who I had bumped into at a previous service we had. It wasn't hard to remember who she was talking about because she stayed in my spirit. We looked at each other (the woman I bumped into) and I said, "You look familiar." She smiled and said, "So do you." We both knew we had never met before. We smiled and went our separate ways. Evangelist Booker said that woman is a Prophetess and God has given her a word for you concerning your husband, so hold on. I said to myself, I knew there was some kind of connection to that woman. It didn't cross my mind to ask Evangelist Booker if she had her number. That evening I prayed that God would allow me to meet her again.

Those Who Wait On GOD

Chapter #15

Nicole

A Word From The Lord

I went to church that Sunday feeling as though my life was about to change. As the word went forth I happened to look to my right and there she was! The Prophetess that I bumped into! I knew this was my answer from God. I didn't think I would see her again. Now that she was here I was not going to leave without speaking to her. This wasn't about being thirsty for a word. I knew that this meeting was divine and ordained by God. After church was over, I went to her and before I could say a thing she said, "I have to talk to you." She told me her name was Donine and to get her number from Evangelist Booker and I did. When I called Prophetess Donine the first thing she said was, "Woman of God, the young man you were going to marry was not it. He was "The Counterfeit!"

I immediately began to cry. I didn't feel like he was my husband, but I just needed to know for sure so that I wasn't wasting time. It wasn't that I wanted this man so bad either. I just wanted to be in the will of God; even if it meant to wait on a man who had gone on to be in another relationship. Thank God for revealing to me that He did not intend for me to go through all of this! It felt so good to know that I wasn't crazy and that God was actually speaking to me and sending warning all this time! She went on to tell me that my husband was also waiting for his wife (me) and that he was in school. She described his features and went on to say that he was very handsome, but he would have eyes for only me. She said he was taller than me and I almost ran through the house because I said, "Lord, please let him be taller than me with heels on!" It wasn't just a superficial thing.

It was just what I liked and at times when you desire to be in the will of God you began to pray and desire his will for your life anyway. Yes! God is into details! The enemy isn't the only one to send what you like. It's just that with God, He knows what we "need" is more important! It was just so overwhelming. She didn't just tell me things I wanted to hear, but these were things God placed in my spirit even before I met Jason, so I knew it was God! God used her to tell me that I would meet my husband before the year 2008 was out. That we would know God was in the union, and that we would be married in 2009! She even said that I needed to start looking at things I wanted for my wedding.

She said the reason we were going to marry so quickly was because of the work the Lord had for us to do. She told me that he was going to go to school to get his Master's Degree in Theology. I knew this was God because she also shared personal things with me that nobody knew. God heard my prayers! Not only did He have someone set aside just for me, but we were like minded and I was going to meet him next year! My faith instantly clicked in. That's all I needed! God encouraged me so much by using this vessel. Now that I knew what God was doing I began to target my prayers. I prayed that God would bind us together. I prayed that there would be a supernatural connection even though we had not met yet.

I prayed that we would be on one accord even though I had not talked to him or knew who he was. I asked God to place his needs in my spirit in order to teach me to pray, not for a husband, but the one God specifically set aside just for me! It fell in my spirit to sow a monetary seed for his finances in which I gave along with my tithes and offerings.

I wrote on the back of my tithing envelope for my house and my husband. This was no voodoo or witchcraft. I was led by the spirit of the Lord to do this. I was not doing these things to get a husband; I realized God had already chosen one for me. I had a vision years ago that I was pulling up to a single family home that sat alone. I remember a driveway as well but I didn't park on it. I parked in front of the house. In this vision I had my nails freshly manicured with French tips. I believe I had just come from the nail salon.

My pastor at the time told me that she felt God would give me an apartment, but I kept seeing this house. So I believed God for it and I included it on the back of my tithing envelope. I know they probably thought I was crazy because clearly I was single and living with my father. But this was an act of faith tied with obedience. I was so excited about what God was doing. There was no more confusion! I was reminded that God always wanted what was best for me and the hurt I endured (although some of which was self-inflicted) could not be compared to the love the Father had for me. God assured me that He was healing my heart and preparing me for His son.

All of the pain associated with my test and trials served a purpose!

One morning I was getting ready for work and the Holy Spirit said, "Pray! Your husband believes someone else is his wife." I then said out loud, "The devil is a lie! I know I didn't wait all this time to go through this!" So I ignored the voice and began to iron my clothes. However, I was up extra early and had time to sit down and think. I was a little disturbed by what fell in my spirit. Then my phone rung and it was Prophetess Donine.

Her exact words were "Woman of God you need to pray! You have not come yet and your husband thinks someone else is his wife!" I began to weep as I told her the Lord just placed the same thing in my spirit and I tried to dismiss it. She said, "No, God is intertwining you with him even now to know what to pray for concerning him." We went to the Lord, for my husband whom I did not know. She led the prayer and began to bind the spirit of confusion!

Those Who Wait On GOD

Chapter #16

Nicole

You Don't Date?

I was not entertaining anyone that I felt God was saying not to and this time I meant business! It seemed as though everybody and their grandfather wanted to come out of the woods! My pastor had to preach at another church and after service was over a young man came up to me and introduced himself as the host pastor's son. He went on to tell me that he went to my pastor concerning me. Finally he came out with it and asked if I was interested in talking outside of church. He said that he was attracted to my "anointing". "Thank you..." I said. "But I am not lead to start dating at this time."

My pastor even asked me why I wasn't dating and I told her that I was waiting on God to send my spouse. It seemed like everyone I talked to was not convinced. Even people in the church had a hard time understanding my decision. I was told that I would never find or receive what I was looking for, that I should just go ahead and become a nun and any guy willing to wait until marriage was probably under cover (not interested in woman); even people on my job began to ask questions. One day one of the men at the office came to get a peppermint off my desk; he was trying to make small talk. "Are you seeing anyone?" He asked. When I said no he said, "Are you interested in seeing someone?" I gave him the same response – "No." This thoroughly confused him, so he went on to ask if I was a lesbian. "Most certainly not," I replied.

These responses were not enough. "Well why aren't' you dating?" He continued. I told him that I was waiting on God and he gave me the same response everyone gave me. He said, "Then how will you find a husband if you don't date?" I told him that I won't find him that the word of God says in Proverbs 18:22, "He who finds a wife finds a good thing, and obtains favor from the Lord." So I don't have to find him. He will find me. "Well, how will you know who it is when he approaches you, if he approaches you?" He asked. When I replied, "God will place it in my spirit that it's him." He said, "Okay, Good luck." People simply could not wrap their brains around my decision. One young lady asked how I could even consider marrying a man without sleeping with him first. I told her I trust God even in that area!

I prayed to Him concerning everything. I said God knows my sexual desires and that's not the most important thing on the list. I thought that way when I was led by my own fleshly desires and it got me nowhere. It had me bound! I was no longer just looking for him to be tall, handsome and educated, but saved, sanctified, delivered and attached to the purpose God had for my life! Others went as far as to suggest that what I believed God for was just too big of a job. Some said that God didn't put people together; that there were options, but all I could do was speak for myself! I know what instructions God gave me to follow and it was according to my faith! There was no doubt in my mind that He would lead me and do what He said!

This experience also taught me that when you are trying to do anything for God you will face opposition. When you are trying to live for God you will be tested and tried. Some things that you are tempted by are a result of what's already in you.

The word of God says in James 1:14, "But every man is tempted, when he is drawn away of his own lust, and enticed." That is why it is important that we keep this flesh under subjection by praying, fasting and reading God's word. If I did not have a personal relationship with God it would have been difficult to stand the test I was to face and to trust God to carry me through it all!

Those Who Wait On GOD

Chapter #17

Nicole

Breaking The Soul Tie

I was totally over Jason and the entire situation. I was now praying for my husband and I was excited about our meeting because it was now the year 2008! I knew this was the year we would meet as God used the woman of God to say! I held onto that word! I searched for a wedding dress as she advised, but I did not lose focus. I was so content with being single. I would go to dinner alone and while eating I would write out my prayers in a journal I purchased. I remember writing about how I never really did anything special for Valentine's Day or for my birthday. Since they were both in February, I thought it would be awesome if I could be married in the month of February as well. In my private times praying, I expressed that I wanted to leave our wedding reception and go right to our honeymoon. I wanted to go to Rome, Italy as I thought it would be romantic and different.

I was just sharing my thoughts with God. I was ready to meet this man that the enemy tried so hard to keep me from! I wondered if he was experiencing this much warfare besides believing someone else was "it" as well. I decided that night I would say a special prayer for him, as if he was already walking alongside me. I would pray for his strength not just to wait for me but for the ability to stand and that he would be pleasing to God. Whenever you are close to your blessing, expect something to come in to try and interrupt what God is doing. Out of the blue, Rick called (my ex - the one I met on a chat line and dated on and off for years). He got my number from one of his cousins who I was close with. I didn't recognize the number, after answering and hearing his voice I thought to myself, here we go... again.

I knew for sure he wasn't my husband because we were headed in two different directions and I don't mean physically. I mean spiritually. I knew that this was a distraction, but every time he came around I just gave in. The soul tie was strong; it was like I was drawn to him. I knew I had no business seeing him but once again, after doing so well I found myself going backwards. There was no mistake or confusion. This was a soul tie that had to be broken once and for all. Even if I still had feelings for this guy I had to be able to pass the test this time! I knew that the enemy wanted to pull me out of position, but I was weak. I thought I had control over the situation, but I was just deceiving myself. We went from just talking on the phone to him eventually asking me to meet him in public places and I agreed.

One time in particular he asked me to meet him at a "lounge". Well when I got to the "lounge" I realized it was more like a bar. I immediately felt convicted, but I stayed anyway convincing myself that it was o.k. because I wasn't there to drink. Actually what I was doing was compromising. He began to play a game of pool and I stood behind him. This woman came to the table drunk out her mind. She was talking slurred and could hardly stand.

I wanted to go over and minister to her, but then realized that I was there – in the bar with her. I felt like I had no right to minister to her because I was creeping across town with a man that I knew was not my husband. The enemy tries to shut your mouth and make you feel like you are not worthy and it worked that night. I didn't say a thing! I felt so bad, why was I there?! I felt like I was drowning, but I convinced myself I was alright because I hadn't sunk yet. After all, I still went to church no matter how late I got in the house from hanging out with him, and at this point I was hanging out with him every Saturday and now even during the week. Romans 7:19 says, "For the good that I would I do not: but that evil which I would not, that I do."

Every time I said I would not do a thing I found myself doing it anyway. I even prayed a ridiculous prayer like God kill me if I mess up again. I am so glad He didn't answer that one because here I was again…compromising! I was doing the things that I knew was displeasing to God to gratify my fleshly desires. We sometimes make the mistake of blaming "the fall" on someone else but like I stated earlier with scripture to support it, we are tempted by our own desires. We went from talking on the phone to him and I spending weekends together and I felt so ashamed! I couldn't believe that with all this word, speaking in tongues, gifts and power…I was in this situation again!

I thought I was in control, but that's how the enemy makes you feel. You say to yourself, 'I got this. I am only going this far. I am only talking on the phone. I am only going to the movies with him or her. I am only stopping by. I am only…" Suddenly, the "only's" lead you back into bondage! The bible refers to the same as a dog returning to its own vomit (2 Peter 2:22). The enemy isn't concerned with you falling because he knows you have a chance to be forgiven. He wants to wipe you out and make you believe that your destiny will not be fulfilled because of what you have done! We know that God forgives, but we still reap the consequences (the law of sowing and reaping) of our actions. This is why He gives us instructions.

The bible isn't about a bunch of rules to follow. He sets guidelines so that we won't have to go through unnecessary hurt. For instance, you had a baby before marriage. You are forgiven! God will still use you mightily! He did not and will not take away the gifts in you and you are still anointed (chosen by God)! The thing is, because of the decision you made you are now connected to someone for the rest of your life that you may feel isn't going in the same direction you are headed in. Maybe at the time you didn't have a personal relationship with God. Maybe at the time you did not understand the importance of having been directed by God in reference to a father for your children. Now you are concerned about your child going to the other parent's house because maybe his or her life reflects where you were, but the good thing is God has them!

Romans 8:28 says, "And we know that in all things God works for the good of those who love him, who have been called according to his purpose." The enemy has messed up when he tries to entrap those who love God. The mess you made will become a testimony of God's love, mercy and His grace! Your testimony will put you in a position to minister to the people of God who have found themselves in the same situation you were once in! They will be set free and God will get all of the glory! So this is why you must continue to press and ignore the thoughts in your mind that speak against the word of God; reciting that you can't serve Him, that you have gone too far and have done too much! Sometimes you get sick of yourself! You get sick of making a declaration every year, month or week that you will be free; but you need to realize that there is Power in your words! "Ye are of God....and have over-come them: because greater is he that is in you, than he that is in the world" (1 John 4:4).

I didn't fully realize all that just yet! All the boundaries I had set with others just went out the window when it came to him. I was ironing my clothes, getting ready for another evening out with Rick and I started to cry. I was thinking to myself, Nicole what is it going to take?! I am falling deeper and deeper into sin messing with this man. We are not headed in the same direction and we keep coming into each other's life with no purpose. I realized he was becoming a hindrance to me and an Idol because I was placing him before God! I then asked God, "What is it going to take to free me?!" Just then God spoke to me and said, "Your love for me. That's what it will take." I began to think about where God brought me from. How God loved me and cleaned me up after he and other men were gone and out of my life.

I began to think about how God kept and covered me the months I had no car and provided a way back and forth to work. I began to think about how He anointed me and used me to be a blessing to so many people - even on my job. I thought about my love for God and how it was worth severing any ties to anyone or anything that would assist me in disappointing Him. It all came down to a decision and I chose God. Yes, I wanted to meet my husband, but God wanted me to choose Him first. He wanted my choice to be based off my love for Him, not because I was to meet another man (my husband that year). If I did it because I wanted a husband, I would have carried this man (Rick) in my heart and in my thoughts going into marriage.

Galatians 5:1 then fell in my spirit! "Stand fast therefore in the liberty wherewith Christ hath made us free, and be not entangled again with the yoke of bondage." I began to weep and repent. I told the Lord that I would serve Him wholeheartedly and I didn't care who it was or what it was – nothing was going to separate me from Him! That evening Rick called and he apologized for causing me any grief early on in our relationship, as he and I were both young. He then said, "I know that your husband is coming." I looked at the phone in disbelief. He then expressed that he was a little jealous, but he knew that he was going to marry as well. I knew then that I had to come out and say it. I couldn't beat around the bush. I had to let him know that we could no longer talk. This situation was past getting married!

He clearly said, "I know you aren't my wife," so what was the purpose of "chilling?" I told him that I wanted what God had for me and that we could not talk anymore. With that, the calls immediately stopped. I even changed my cell number which is something I would have never done. I would always leave the door cracked, but this time I realized that nobody ever did me better than Jesus. No man was worth my salvation, my purpose and who God was preparing me to be! I thought to myself, this feels so good! Now I can finally move forward!

Those Who Wait On GOD
Chapter #18
Tony
What God Has For You

It was now spring 2008 and the thorn was still in my side. The pain of knowing what I had prayed for didn't happen. I remember going to bible study and my bishop was led by the spirit to say, "Sometimes we do not know why God may allow a thing to happen, but we just need to let it go and not question it." In that moment, I lifted my head towards heaven and with all the strength in me I said "Lord, I let it go." From that point forward the weight was lifted and I was free. Although the thorn over this entire situation was gone I still felt down, but I didn't really know why.

During this time I was off work because of an injury to my back and neck. Consequently, I had some idle time to reflect over my life. One Friday, I was lying on the floor in my house and it was as if a light bulb came on in my spirit; "the fire I previously had for God was gone." This is why we have to pray and commune with God. If I didn't know any better, I would have thought I wasn't delivered because of the feeling of weariness trying to overtake me.

That evening after Bible study our choir had to sing at another church. However, I had a committee meeting for our upcoming youth conference that I had to attend. Therefore, I wasn't going to sing with the choir because this was our initial meeting and I felt I needed to be there. But, let me tell you how God will orchestrate things when it is time for you to receive your blessing, there is no way you will miss it! What He has for you is for you!

Right before I went into the meeting I received a phone call from our choir directress saying that she needed me to come to the church to sing with the choir. I should have known this was God because it wasn't like I was a soloist. I could hold a note, but that's about it. Trust me; the choir would have been just fine without me. Nonetheless, I was excused from the meeting and I went to sing with my fellow choir members.

After our choir sang, a few of my friends (Rob and Jay) and I just hung around because there was nothing else to do. Towards the end of the night, Rob looked over at the refreshment table and happened to see this beautiful young lady. He tapped me and said, "Look". When I looked she was very nice looking and she appealed to me immediately. The crazy part is I didn't see her face, just her side profile. Rob then said he was going to get her number. I said, "No you're not. I am!" Although, I said it, I didn't move. I just observed her.

She had a glow, I felt in my spirit that she was a Proverbs 31 woman; it was something about her that was different than the average female. I didn't know then, but thinking back, it was the anointing. Not that I have never seen or met other anointed women, but this time the anointing was familiar.

It reflected mine. Before I knew it some of the choir members became aware of the fact that I had my eyes on her. Of course, a few people began to press me to go and speak to her, but I just didn't feel in my spirit to do so. That doesn't mean I did nothing. I asked another young lady from the choir to go and ask her if she was dating. When the young lady returned she said, "She told me that she is not interested and that she was waiting on her husband".

What!? Wait! If you remember a few chapters ago I stated, "I used to tell women that I was waiting on my wife". Let me tell you, what God has for you is for you! Suppose I had left God and went back to the club life! My wife was not in the club – this is why it is important for you to be sensitive to the spirit. God will direct you right to your blessing.

A lot of people always ask, "How do you know when someone is the one?" I really cannot answer that for you because every situation is different. But what I can say is that when you are connected to God and He is connected to your future spouse and the both of you are in tune with the spirit, there is no way you will miss each other. That's why it's important to commune with the Lord and have a relationship with Him first.

Obviously, when I heard she was waiting on her husband I was amazed and in awe. I still wasn't led to approach her at that time. When we left the church, they were still trying to get me to go back and ask for her number. I was tempted, but my spirit pressed me to say no. Out of nowhere I told my friends, "We will come back Sunday and I will ask her then." Just then they agreed to come back with me.

On the way home I could not get this woman out of my spirit. Jay and Rob were having a conversation - supposedly with me - but I was in outer space. Jay then says to me "You're thinking about her aren't you"? And undeniably I said, "Yes. We have to go back Sunday!" When God is truly directing you, be sure to do your part or it won't work. Please be sure that you are being directing by God first; you saw what happened to me early on.

Those Who Wait On GOD
Chapter #19
Nicole

I'm Not Interested

My friend Maria always had her hands in something in the kingdom. This time Maria planned a night of worship at our church. It would be held on a Friday night and different choirs and praise teams were scheduled to minister. As she planned, she asked if I would come and help. The day of the event it was raining and I felt a little under the weather, but I pressed my way because she'd asked me to be there. I stopped at the market to get some things so I wouldn't have to stop at the end of the event; I knew that it would probably end late. I was in line waiting to purchase my items and it fell in my spirit to look at a little stand behind me that had different books on it.

I never purchased a book from the market before, and had no idea they sold spiritual books. It then fell in my spirit to go over to the book stand. I was already in line; in fact I was the next customer. Determined to be obedient, I got out of line and looked at the books and my eyes zoomed in on a book called, "The Gifts of the Holy Spirit." I purchased it and kept moving. I'd brought my clothes with me and changed in the basement of the church. I was sleepy and trying to get myself together, nevertheless I was glad that I pressed my way.

I saw Prophetess Donine and decided I would sit with her the duration of the event. We were discussing how good

God was and how great the event turned out. After we finished talking, I got up to set up the food table. While walking back to my seat a young lady approached me and says, "There's a young man here and he is interested in meeting you. He did not want to be disrespectful in case you were seeing someone and he was here. So he asked me to come over." There was absolutely no way I was going through any more drama! I was sticking to how I asked God for it to happen. While in prayer I said to God, "I don't want to meet him at a church event, gas station or outing." I felt that my husband was coming to "get me" and would approach me at church.

Even though we were in church, I was looking for that connection in my spirit. I decided that my prayers would also be my "prophecy". I made so many wrong choices in the past. I prayed and asked God to reveal things and He did. I believed that God would honor my prayer by allowing my husband to come the way I asked, so I would be sure. My prayer being answered would rule out if he was a counterfeit! With that being said, I told her I was not interested. She then said "He is right over there would you at least like to look at him?" I told her, "No, I am not interested in seeing him either. I am waiting on God for my husband." The young lady said, "Okay," and she walked away. I didn't even look back.

I went back to my seat and told Prophetess Donine what happened. I told her that someone was trying to holler and I sent the message back that I was not interested, because I was waiting on God for my husband. She said I know that's right and we gave each other a high five. It was not a game! I was not getting caught up in any mess again! I stuck to my guns as they say, but little did I know this night was just the beginning of a beautiful testimony.

Those Who Wait On GOD

Chapter #20
Sunday Morning

Nicole's version

The event on Friday night was awesome! Now here comes Sunday, which was also Mother's Day. As I said in the beginning I lost my mom at a young age. I always took it well, but for some reason I was feeling a bit down that day. I was going to visit a sister's in Christ church instead of mine, but just then my spiritual mom called me and said that I needed to be at church a little early because this Sunday they were calling for the combined praise team- so that meant I had to sing.

Tony's Version

Sunday morning came rather quickly but I was ready...so I thought. Rob, Jay and another friend, James went with me just as they said they would. We pulled up to the church, walked to the door and I froze. I thought about leaving and going to my home church. I had Jay on one side saying, "Let's go in," and Rob on the other side saying, "Let's go home." James, who was also with us, didn't care what we did. Jay finally took control of the situation and led the way inside the sanctuary and we followed. As we went in to sit down, I saw her standing in the front of the church; she was singing on the praise team. The butterflies came back, but I blocked that out and began to worship God. After the praise team sat down the pastor approached the podium.

103

She began to speak to the single women and then asked them to stand. Nicole was among those standing. The pastor took it a step further and said, "Some of your husbands are coming very soon." Jay turned around and looked at me and we both started laughing. After about three hours into the service the -pastor then said, "Let's get to the Word." With the most amazed look on my face I thought, "You have to be kidding me. My home church family is probably home eating right now." We had already been in here for the last three hours. I must be on "Punk'd". Where are the cameras? I have to admit this was one of the longest services I had ever sat in. I thought to myself she better be "the one" after sitting in this long service. Nonetheless, the Word came forth and ironically the passage of scripture was Proverbs 31.

Upon the end of the service I became nervous all over again. I hesitated for a second, but I finally got up the guts to go over to her. As I began walking towards her I noticed she was speaking with another person, but as I got closer she was standing alone. As I approached her she began moving out of the way to let me pass. She was oblivious to the fact that I had come for her. I introduced myself and told her that I was not one of these Pentecostal pimps who prey on females in the church. She laughed. I proceeded with letting her know that I was a college graduate with my own house and job.

I was building my case so she would know that this eagle could carry her weight. It really didn't matter what weight I could carry because when I asked her for her name and number, she said, "Nicole, but I don't give my number out to men. Maybe we will see each other at the next church event." I said, "Okay, when is the next church event?" She said, "The end of June." Huh? It was the beginning of May.

I almost pleaded because it seemed like a long time. But she did not change her response.

After going through all the motions of being a gentleman, she further says, "I have to minister to this sister that is waiting for me." In other words, good day sir! Honestly, I was not mad, but I did feel like time was wasted . . . so I thought.

Nicole's Version

While singing I noticed a group of young men coming in the church, but I didn't pay much attention. When we sat down my pastor at the time began to talk about a virtuous woman; she said that some of the singles were about to get married and even asked us (the single ladies) to stand up. I was a little embarrassed but I was obedient. Once service was over I noticed a young man walking towards me. I moved so that he could get pass, but as he got closer I felt that he was going to approach me. He did. In fact he introduced himself. He said his name was Tony, just then I was ready to give my speech until he said, "I am the young man from Friday." Right then and there I felt this "strange" connection. It was not one due to a physical attraction, although he was very attractive. It was one that I had never felt before so I couldn't quite put my finger on it. He then asked if we could exchange numbers; however I didn't want to give out my number.

I was still sticking to not speaking with anyone unless I knew I was being led by God and in that case he had to be my husband; the one God sent. I then asked if we could plan on meeting at a youth event that my church was having at the end of June. He said, "I didn't plan on waiting that long, but o.k." I wasn't trying to be a hard case but he did not know my story and he didn't have to know. The only reason I asked if he would like to come then was because of this connection I felt. If we were going to see each other again it would not be on a date. It would be among other young people in a group setting and not an intimate one. I didn't want any misunderstandings. Just then I saw a young lady that had been going through some things trying to get my attention. I told him that I really needed to talk with her as she had been standing there waiting for a while. I was also beginning to feel like all eyes were on us as well. So I told him that I had to attend to her and with that we said our goodbyes.

After ministering to the sister and leaving the church, Maria and I went to see a play. The entire time we were there I kept thinking about the young man (who I now knew as Tony) approaching me at church. Of course I told him that I wanted to meet him at the next church event and I was sure about that, but I just could not get him out of my spirit. I expressed this to Maria and she said, "Well, he might be your husband." I quickly said to Maria that every man who is attractive is not a husband and we both laughed.

My stomach and my head began to hurt and I thought that it was because I had been fasting. Maria was next to me texting. She then turned and asked if I wanted to go out to eat with a group of young people from Friday night's event. I said sure. She saw that I looked a little uncomfortable and asked was I okay and if I was sure that I wanted to go? I assured Maria that I was fine and that I was just hungry and probably needed to get something to eat. After the play ended we headed over to the restaurant to fellowship and have a bite to eat.

Tony's Version

After that long service Rob and I went back to my house just to hang out because it was raining outside. Ironically, Rob receives a text from Maria who was actually with Nicole at the time. She asked Rob if we wanted to meet them at a restaurant in Canton. Rob then asked me if I wanted to go. I was hesitant because of the weather and on top of that my head and stomach was hurting. But I agreed to go anyway. Rob and I got to the restaurant first and Nicole and Maria came minutes later.

I could tell Nicole was rather agitated before they got to the table. Come to find out Maria did not tell Nicole that it was just Rob and I at the restaurant. Nicole was under the impression that it was a group of young people from the event. As we began to talk during dinner, Nicole said that she was apprehensive about coming because her head and stomach was hurting prior to them arriving to the restaurant. This was getting weirder by the minute because earlier my stomach and head was hurting as well.

Nicole's Version

As we are walking into the restaurant I was surprised to see the young man who approached me at church earlier that day and his friend sitting at the table. I was NOT happy! I looked at Maria and said, "What is this?! You know I am not dating!" This looked suspiciously like a double date. I told him that I would see him at the next church event and suddenly we are about to have dinner. I told myself o.k. Nicole, take a chill pill.

You didn't come with the intent on seeing him. You are eating and that's it. I sat down and said hello to Tony and his friend. Seeing him sitting at the table, I got nothing that said this is your boo! I sat there thinking, I cannot believe this! I felt like I was bamboozled! I know some of you are like she is acting real deep! If you go back a few pages you'll understand why I was determined that THIS time I was not doing it my way or anyone else's! I was going to be led by God this time and I was not going to let him down. As for right now all I could do was sit, eat and engage in this conversation.

Tony's Version

During dinner we began to discuss different things and she actually told me my calling. She told me that I was going to be a pastor. "She tripping," I thought to myself. I had no desire to be a pastor, but I did want to be a judge in the court of law. Deep inside I knew she was correct, but I just laughed as if it was a figment of her imagination. I actually wanted it to be a figment of my imagination, but it was destined. After the awesome dinner, we stood outside the restaurant doors and prayed. The Glory of God fell on the four of us, Rob was on the ground and the rest of us just invoked God's presence. Before we knew it two hours had passed and seemingly every store in the area was closed.

We all left feeling good about the presence of God. I almost forgot about Nicole. Actually I didn't, but I thought if it is meant to be then it will be. I didn't have time for any bootleg relationships that would have gotten me nowhere. On my way to drop Rob off home he received a phone call from Maria saying to put me on the phone. When I received the phone it was Nicole on the other end saying what an awesome time she had, that she perceived that I was a man of God. "Well Lord, I am not sure what you are doing, but keep going," I laughed to myself.

Nicole's Version

The food was great and the conversation was as well! We talked about so many different things. It was so refreshing to talk with other young people who understood the struggle of staying on the right track but being determined to please God! At one point in the conversation Tony said he didn't really know what his calling was. I interjected and said, "You know what your calling is. You are called to Preach, you will be a pastor." He looked at me as to say how did you know, and you are tripping all at the same time!

We were so engaged in the conversation that the restaurant was now closing; in fact they began vacuuming all around us. I thought that was odd, they let us continue to sit and talk. Tony and his friend, being gentlemen, were concerned about our safety and decided that we should get ready to leave as it was getting late. I was going to ask if we could all pray first, but Tony took the words right out of my mouth.

After praying the heavens down we left. While getting in the car it fell in my spirit, "He doesn't know if you are interested." "Should he know?" I questioned within myself. It then fell in my spirit to call him and let him know that I enjoyed the fellowship. I asked Maria if she would call the gentleman so that I could speak with Tony. When he was on the line I told him that I really enjoyed the fellowship. Tony said, "Okay," and with that we hung up.

It fell in my spirit that he was going to call back and he did. We spoke the entire ride to Maria's house. When Tony got to his house he asked if he could call me from his phone because we were still on his friend's phone. I didn't feel the need to hesitate, so I gave him my number being as though I was on Maria's phone as well. We talked until I got home safely. When I was home we said good night and established that we would talk later.

Those Who Wait On GOD

Chapter #21
Lord Is This You?

Nicole... While at Work

The next morning I went to work early so that I could pray at my desk. While in prayer I said, "Lord I gave this man my number! I told you that I was not entertaining anyone that was not my husband. Why did it fall in my spirit to call him? Please lead me." Right in the midst of my prayer it fell in my spirit to fast with him for three days. I then said aloud, "I am not asking him that Lord. If it is meant for us to fast then you will have to place it in his spirit. I am done with telling the counterfeit the plans I have or what "You" have for me so they can make me believe or even convince themselves that they are the one." After my prayer, I decided to go on a fast that day and end it at 6pm. I also said to God that I knew Tony was going to call me. If he did not bring up the fast I was going to tell him that it was better if we did not talk. We would just stick with the plan of meeting each other at the next youth event.

Tony's Version...The Phone Call

In my prayer closet, actually in my den earlier that Monday I heard the word "fire" in my spirit three times. Not paying it any mind, I went ahead with my day. That evening, Nicole and I talked on the phone for almost eight hours. At the end of our conversation the Lord placed in my spirit for us to pray and fast for three days to seek confirmation of our relationship. Surprisingly her response was, "SHUT

111

UP!" I responded in a confused manner saying, "Huh?" Finally she explained to me that she was in awe because earlier that day while she was at work the Lord told her to do the same. She said that she asked God to tell me because she did not want to ask me herself. Ultimately, Nicole and I were concerned about this connection if it was not God's will. At this time in our lives, we had both been through hell and high water believing that we previously found our spouses.

So now, it was time out for foolishness. Point blank, God is this you?! If not, we need to say God bless and keep it moving. One thing that I realized is that you have to be careful who you date and marry. Believers think that just because the other person is saved God approves of the relationship. We should always desire to be in God's divine Will. Why cheat yourself and settle for less just because you believe you have been waiting too long? Who are we to tell God when, what and how He should do things for us? The truth of the matter is He does not have to do anything. So, be patient and wait. Don't move ahead of Him and do it yourself. Why settle and reap the sinner's reward and have to start over from where He originally wanted you to start in the first place?

Nicole's Version... The Phone Call

Monday evening Tony called as I expected and it was just as I was ending my fast. We talked about God and how we were truly living for Him at this point and time in our lives. I came to find that Tony had actually given his life to the Lord in 2005 which was the same year I did. I thought that was awesome, but I still wasn't playing any games. I knew what I had asked God and if I did not get it, we could not talk on the phone anymore. The more you talk to someone, the more you begin to take an interest and I did not want an emotional attachment to someone who was not my husband.

Once an emotional attachment is formed the tendency is to settle or even ignore signs that the person may not be the one for you. People have spent years in a relationship that they weren't supposed to be in because they overlooked things and situations. They allowed themselves to commit because they simply liked the person. Wrongful relationships are not just abusive or where the couple is unequally yoked, but you can both be saved and be outside the will of God. The question is, are they connected to your God given purpose?! A person's looks or lineage (being the son or daughter of a pastor) doesn't qualify him or her either. I wanted to know what God said about him and I wanted God's approval.

After talking for some hours it was now 9pm. He said he was going to let me go so I could be well rested for work the next day. I thought that was very nice. He wasn't trying to be on the phone until the wee hours of the morning. He wanted me to get rest. He then said, "Let's pray before we get off the phone." I said, "Okay," with the intention of telling him we could no longer talk as soon as he finished. While he was praying I had Israel & New Breed's song "Grace" playing. Tony started praying down the heavens and he kept praying all these prayers of protection. As he prayed I felt led to go to my father's room door and lay my hand on it. As I did this Tony began to pray for God's protection over my dad. He must have remembered me telling him that I lived with him.

After Tony ended the prayer he said, "As I was praying it fell in my spirit for us to fast together for three days." Now you can imagine my surprise! I didn't mean it but I said out loud, "SHUT UP!" Again, I didn't mean to tell him to shut up, and I didn't literally mean shut up, but I was taken back like, "WHAT?!" I did not come to the conclusion just then that this was my husband. I thought to myself, God is something else. "Why did you tell me to shut up?" Tony asked. I told him about my conversation with God earlier and how I had already started my fast and ended it when he called. There was a moment of silence and he then said, "Wow." We then established that during the fast we were not going speak to each other. We were going to seek God in reference to the purpose of our meeting and with that we ended the conversation.

Tony's Version... The Fast

Early Tuesday morning I received a text from Nicole telling me that her apartment caught on fire. Remember "fire" fell in my spirit three times the day before. Ironically, Nicole was really calm and we went forward with the fast. We did not speak to each other during the three day fast because we wanted to clearly hear from God without the influence of our flesh. During this period, I was before the throne of grace like never before. I prayed, "God, you have blessed me to get to an awesome place in you. I do not want to mess that up by getting involved in a relationship that was not orchestrated by You. If this is not it, Father, please let me know because I don't want to go through this again." However, God began to confirm what He had already started. I remember during the fast I went to church for choir rehearsal and I told one of the elders that I needed to speak to him about something.

This particular elder has a strong prophetic gift and out of nowhere he said, "I hope she doesn't go here." Meaning he hoped I was over the situation with India, as she had moved on. I said "No." We laughed. Again, I was a little amazed because I did not disclose to him what I wanted to talk about, but at this point I began to pay attention to every little detail. He then says, "Your spouse will be able to tell you what your calling is…." Wow, this was even more confirmation because I never told the elder that Nicole told me what my calling was at dinner two days ago. Despite all of this confirmation, at the end of the fast I did not have a final word from God that this was it. Nevertheless I remained prayerful.

Nicole's Version… The Fast

The first day of the fast it seemed as if all hell was breaking loose. I went to sleep with Israel & New Breed's song "Grace" playing on repeat. It was about 6am when a very faint sound woke me up. I didn't hear any music playing so I used the remote to the radio player and it would not work. I then tried to turn on the television and that would not work either. So I called out to my father. I wanted to see if he was awake and if he knew what was going on. I then heard my dad holler. He ran from his bedroom to the kitchen. While in the kitchen he grabbed a few empty gallons of milk jugs and began to fill them with water.

I ran into his room to see what had him so frantic. As I entered his room I saw that the entire frame of his bed was in flames. He began to run back and forth as the house filled up with smoke. Very quickly I picked up my keys, cell phone, put on my shoes and grabbed my purse. I told my dad we had to get out of there. As we sat outside, we watched the fire men take an ax to break the windows. I looked over and saw tears coming down my father's face. I hadn't seen him cry since my mother passed away. He said, "I don't know what I am going to do." I comforted him and said, "Trust God daddy." I then text Tony and told him what took place.

He text back saying that "fire" fell in his spirit the day before. I now understood why he prayed for protection and why I was led to lay hands on my father's bedroom door. With that, I thanked him for his prayers and we continued with the fast. My sister let me stay with her during this time. My job also had a policy that allowed exactly three days off due to a fire. This was even more confirmation that we were both hearing God clearly and going in the right direction. I didn't understand all that was going on, but as long as I was in the will of God, I knew I was in a safe place. I gathered the things I could salvage. My sister was at work so I had time to sit and pray. I began to pray for my Dad and then started focusing on the meaning of all that was happening. Just then I said to myself, why would God place it in Tony's spirit that there would be a fire and not mine? It was obvious that God was already connecting us. I also thought of the times I prayed and asked God to reveal to me things about my husband. Through prayer God shared with me that my husband would operate in the prophetic as well. I didn't know why God was sharing that with me at the time. I was just excited to know anything about this man that I was going to meet.

On day two of the fast, I prayed and asked God to allow me to walk in His purpose and that His perfect will would be done in my life. I began to think about what had taken place so far. I knew that God would not place in my spirit to fast with a man who was not my husband, because there is a difference between fasting for a person and fasting with a person. I was not lead to fast for him, for his deliverance or for his healing. There was no word from the Lord concerning those things. He simply said fast with him. I thought then this may be confirmation that this man could

116

possibly be my husband. I said that I did not want to meet the husband God had for me at a church event and he did not approach me when I sent word back that I was waiting on God to send my spouse.

He then came back to my church to address me himself. That was what I prayed. I didn't want to get ahead of myself. I just took these things as confirmation that I was being guided in the right direction, whatever that was. It then fell in my spirit to read the book that the Holy Spirit led me to purchase from the market the day of the event; where Tony first saw me. As I skimmed through the book I felt strongly that I had to read and study the chapter on, "The Gifts of The Spirit". I didn't know what that had to do with the fast, nonetheless I was obedient. I gained a lot of insight just by reading that one particular chapter. I sat there and began to pray again. I asked God, "O.k. what else should I do?" I never went on a fast in reference to a connection I had to a man; not to mention one that was led by God. While waiting on the leading of the Holy Spirit I began to write down the things I thought he would or should be doing. Now I am supposed to be worrying about myself, but I had too many counterfeits in the past.

Some pretended to want God just to get closer to me. So I wanted to know if he was praying and seeking wisdom or just playing around during this fast. I prayed he was taking this as seriously as I was. I was led to call one of my sisters in Christ (Ms. Adrian) who was an Elder in the church at the time. I told her about the fast I was on and she decided to fast with me that day; so I drove over to her house. She said, "Let us start off with a scripture." She opened the Bible and said that it was the same scripture (Isaiah 58:6) that her and her husband opened to when they were seeking God in reference to their relationship that led to marriage. All I could say was, "Wow." I could see God already moving on this fast, but I was still determined to continue to seek Him.

After we broke the fast, we grabbed a bite to eat. While we were eating she asked if I would like to attend bible study at her church that evening. There was nothing going on at my church, so I agreed to go. After bible study was over, her pastor hugged me. She also prayed for me and said that I was in a season of transition and to continue to seek God. She said I was literally about to pack my bags.

On the last day of the fast it fell in my spirit to go and "spy out the land." I asked God what that meant and He said to visit Tony's church that Sunday. I went on Google to look up his church and read about his Bishop. I instantly felt a connection looking at the picture of the Bishop. It then fell in my spirit to attend Sunday service there; so I wrote down the address. I decided to attend the early service at my church and then attend Tony's church that afternoon.

Tony's Version...Now we can talk

At the end of our fast we called each other anticipating that God gave one of us a direct answer, but it didn't necessarily happen that way. There was no big slap in the face that said here she is! One thing I did pray during the fast was that if Nicole was my wife, I wanted her to be a part of the ministry that I attended. I was a little afraid because I was not sure how this transition was going to take place considering that she was so involved at her church. But, God had it all worked out.

Nicole's Version...Now we can talk

The fast was now over and we were able to speak. We shared what we believed to be confirmation. I was blown when he told me what the Elder at his church said. That was even more confirmation for me. I was now beginning to think, "God could this be him? Is this the man I have been praying and interceding for?" As we continued conversing I told him that at one point in time I believed that someone else was my spouse. He then expressed how he thought that someone else was it as well. Now it was getting even more interesting because I then shared with him how it fell it my spirit that my husband thought that someone else was it and how a sister in Christ and I interceded with prayer.

There was a moment of silence and he said, "Wow!" I also expressed to him that I felt led to visit his church. He was very excited about this. He said that was a part of his prayer during the fast. I was just amazed at God! I still didn't speak out and say to him that he was my husband and he didn't say he knew or even felt like I was his wife. I did feel strongly that it was God's will for us to continue talking and seeking Him every step of the way.

Nicole's Version...Sunday

For the last couple of weeks I had been feeling and hearing that transition was about to take place. I didn't know exactly what God was doing, but I was excited! Sunday morning, I attended early morning service at my church. I arrived at 7:30 am to pray. Usually there was always something I had to do at church but that Sunday, I did not have to minister nor did I have any meetings. I enjoyed the service, which was filled with confirmation. The co-pastor preached on transition! When service was over I headed straight over to Tony's church and when I arrived, the second service was starting; so I was right on time. I walked in the church and I could feel the power of God! As I sat there the Lord began to speak to me loudly. "I am rebuilding you. This is where you belong." While He was speaking to me I noticed the Bishop's voice. It was the same voice I heard while leaving my former church and transitioning to the church I was now attending. I was overwhelmed at this point, I just met this young man and now God was confirming that I was to attend his church. To top it all off, the bishop preached on the gifts of the spirit which is what God had me study during the fast! The book I had purchased from the market - the day Tony saw me, but did not approach me. It was almost like the bishop was reading what I was studying, verbatim. God was putting me in tune with this ministry already.

From there it all started to make sense. He did not approach me the night of the event (at my church) because of my prayer. However, God had Tony in position to see me. Even though all this was coming to me, I was wondering how Tony was going to take it when I told him that I felt God was leading me to attend his church. I didn't want him to think I was just being fast and following him if God had not shown him what he was showing me. After church I sat there waiting for him. He was taking longer than expected so I decided I'd wait in the car. Moments later I received a text asking me my location. I told him I was in the car about to leave. He asked me to wait a moment. Finally, he got in the car and suddenly I felt a little shy. I thought to myself, what in the world is this? Just as I looked up at him I saw a vision of him standing at the end of the aisle (in his church) in a tux. I could not believe what I was seeing!

120

He had to leave, but before he left he expressed that he was glad that I came to the church and would love it if I could come back again to visit. I told Tony that I believed that the Lord was leading me to attend his church. He then said while smiling, "That was my prayer! I prayed that if this was to be then I would like for us to be at the same ministry being poured into by the same pastor." I was so excited that he did not think that I was moving too fast! We also agreed that we were ready to begin the courtship process.

Tony's Version... Sunday

It was now Sunday and Nicole was visiting my church. I was sitting on the choir stand so I could see her clear as day. I was excited! I was standing beside another choir member who I had recently told about Nicole. I said, "She is here!" The funny thing is I never told him what she looked like, but he spotted her out. She had a glow about her. As usual we had a high time in the Lord that day and after the benediction I was still sitting on the pulpit basking in the Lord's presence. After about five to ten minutes I got up and went to the choir room to change out of my robe. When I came back into the sanctuary, Sister Nicole (hilarious) was gone. When I called her she said she was in her car.

I said, "Why did you leave?" "Why did you have me waiting so long?" she replied. I really did not think much of it because this was my normal routine when I had to sing. I went to the back and changed. It was quite obvious that she was upset and I did not understand why at first, but being that she did not know that was my normal routine, her mind was left open to think otherwise. When I got to her car I apologized for not letting her know what I was doing. Then, I tried to give her the Denzel eye. We cleared the air and I asked her to come again sometime as I had to leave for work.

Those Who Wait On GOD

Chapter 22

I Don't Understand

Nicole While At Work

Monday I went to work feeling good! I began praising God because I felt that He was really confirming that this was my husband. He was revealing to me that for once, I was on the right track. I was cleaning the conference room and the tears began to fall. I was saying, "Thank you Jesus" in between every swipe of dust as I wiped off the tables and chairs. When I returned to my desk it fell in my spirit to check my cell phone. I received a text from Tony that blew my mind. Surely God, this was my husband!

Tony - She's At Work

It was Monday morning. I went to the supermarket and while in the meat section I smelled Nicole's perfume which was strange. The scent was very strong; it was as if she was with me. I jokingly sent her a text asking, "Are you in the store where I am?" She worked at least forty minutes from where I was, so I knew that was not the case. I was shocked by her response. The text said, "I was just here praying and thanking God for you at the time you sent the text." In a divine way I believe the Lord was showing us that we were truly connected through Him.

Tony's Version "She Done Got Pulled Up"

Time began to move rapidly. It was my desire that she would be able to join my church. I had no idea how this transition would take place but God works in mysterious ways. There was no wait at all. Nicole started attending my church the very next Sunday. Needless to say, I was happy. When God ordains something He will make the provision for it. Stop trying to figure it out when God already worked it out! Believe that. Although the transition appeared to be quick to me, it felt like a longer process for Nicole.

Nicole's Transition

When I came home from work I received a call from Prophetess Donine. Out of the blue she said, "Now you can let down your guard." I said to myself, "Good Lord!" I had not talked with her. I did not tell her anything about Tony. I knew that before I went to anyone else in reference to him, I needed to hear God for myself and see why He was placing Tony in my spirit. I expressed to her what was taking place. Later, I called Evangelist Booker who had walked with me through this process and I told her everything that had transpired. Finally, I informed one of the young ladies at my church who was in the singles ministry along with me. I told these individuals because I wanted to make sure that I had accountability and prayer throughout the process.

I was anxious to talk to my pastors, but it seemed that someone had beaten me to the punch. The following week I went to bible study, fully intending to schedule a "meeting" with my pastors; however, as I listened to what was being taught I was totally thrown off. I felt as though this was a message concerning me.

It then fell in my spirit to talk to the pastor's wife and tell her everything. I went to her and asked if I could briefly speak with her. As I was telling her about the fast, her husband came over and said that he needed to speak with me. I said, "Okay." He then asked his wife what she and I were discussing and she replied, "The same thing you want to talk to her about." After hearing this he seemed to be somewhat relieved. He then joined in on the conversation. I began to explain to him that I admired him and his wife's relationship. They waited on God as well. I expressed to them that I would love for them to cover me as I begin the courting process with this young man. I told them what happened thus far from the beginning to the end. He said, "Wow! Okay! Well, I want our pastor to meet him." I said, "Okay that's fine. I wanted to talk to her as well, but she had been out of town the entire time this had all transpired."

He then went on to say, "You can tell her, but I don't know what she is going to say. It depends on what is in her spirit." I thought to myself, "That is a strange response." I am making sure I am being held accountable. I knew right then and there that telling her God was leading me to go to his church at any point would possibly be a problem. I wasn't even thinking about leaving soon, maybe after we were engaged, if we were even going to get engaged. I was still seeking God for more confirmation and guidance in the situation. That Sunday the service was awesome and full of more confirmation, but at the latter part of the service I was pulled before the church and told that Tony was not my husband. I spoke to the Senior Pastor and that didn't go well either. As a result of visiting Tony's church, I was released from mine.

I prayed and cried because I had no idea this was the way I would be leaving, but I could not go back. I knew where

God was leading me to go. It was then revealed to me that the fast was to confirm and to prepare me for what was to come. If I hadn't spent time with God I would have thought this was all happening because he was not "The One." I realized just then how important it was to have a personal relationship with God. Now this is not to say that your leader's input on who you are seeing is not needed or valuable. If you have experienced church hurt of any kind, I encourage you to continue in the faith! Don't allow your experiences with man to determine how you will treat God. Have you ever been in a situation where you were friends with a group of people and because one stopped dealing with you they all stopped dealing with you? It was hurtful right?

Well this is how God feels when His children walks away because of someone associated with Him does something wrong to them. God did not do it! He did not cause the offense. If this is you, release what was said or done to you right in this moment. You may feel that this offense should not have come from the one who caused it, but please understand that ALL things work for your good! You are asking, how is it working for my good Nicole? Well look at my testimony. What I experienced positioned me for my blessing! There was purpose in my pain as well as yours!

In the bible, Joseph was betrayed by his own brothers (Genesis 37). He experienced a lot of hurt and rejection from those who were supposed to love him, but it had to happen! Had he not been thrown in the pit, sent to jail and wrongfully accused, his vision would not have come to pass. When God shows us the end of a thing we don't consider the process in getting there. There will be people who are allowed to do some things; forgive them quickly!

126

Would you stay mad at the person who gave you one billion dollars? Would you hate the person(s) that set you up to be blessed? Well then forgive those who have hurt you, lied on you, rejected you and even pushed you out! I say this because had it not happened, you would not have been in position to receive what you have or what is coming! Do not despise the tool or situation God has allowed to usher in your blessing! It is not to kill you, but to set you up for your purpose to be fulfilled!

The following Sunday we went to talk to Tony's bishop. We told him how we met. I then asked if it was o.k. if I joined. He said I was more than welcome to join, not that he would ever decline. I didn't want to just slide in. I wanted to have the talk with him that I couldn't have with my previous pastors. We just wanted some guidance and accountability. It felt like, for the first time in my life, I was sitting under a man of God that was not only full of wisdom, but integrity as well.

Those Who Wait On GOD

Chapter #23

Tony

Wedding Preparation

Tony

Four months lapsed between the time I met Nicole and the time I actually proposed. Ironically, we had already set a wedding date, but I hadn't officially proposed. There was one obstacle that we had to get over. I told Nicole that I highly admire and respect my bishop who is my spiritual father and his approval was necessary. At this point I only knew Nicole for about four to five months and the first thought in my mind was that we were going to have to wait longer, had he not approved.

That Sunday after service I told my bishop that I had to tell him something. Before I could get it out he said, "Ready for the 'I do'?" You talking about shocked! The weight was completely lifted off my shoulders. Waiting on God pays off! When He (God) says "Yes" everything else falls in place. This is why it is important to sit under a pastor who hears from God. People should never take it lightly and disregard the recommendations of their spiritual covering. After my bishop's approval I was ready, so I asked her to marry me on September 7, 2008.

Nicole

All In The Car!

Tony had to go to work in a couple hours, but he still wanted to see me. Of course I said "Yes!" When he arrived he asked if I could come out to his car and sit with him for a little bit until he had to leave. We began discussing possible wedding plans and he hadn't even proposed yet! He stated that he wanted to get married in June and I, not being one who is hard to please was fine with that. Although I prayed that we would get married in the month of February, I was fine with whatever we were going to do; especially since he said it would give us more time to get to know each other.

He also expressed that he wanted to spend our honeymoon on The Freedom of the Seas, the largest cruise ship in the world at the time. I always wanted to go on a cruise ship, so that was fine with me as well. He went on with the plans and stopped mid-way in his conversation and said, "Wait." It was so abrupt I asked, "What's wrong?" He said, "It just fell in my spirit for us to get married in February." I looked so surprised. I said, "You won't believe this, well you probably will . . . My prayer as a single woman was that I wanted to get married in February, sometime around my birthday!"

He said, "WOW!" He then said "Okay, God." When I asked him what was going on, he said, "Would you like to go to Rome, Italy for our honeymoon instead of going on a cruise?" I began to tear up. Tony said, "Are you okay? Don't cry!" I said, "You don't understand. God just keeps confirming that you are truly my husband." I told him how I wrote down that I also wanted to go to Rome, Italy for my honeymoon as well. I couldn't believe how much God was confirming. I can't even explain how good it felt to know that I was in the will of God - especially after ALL the counterfeits. I knew right then and there, this right here was the Real Deal!

Supernatural Provision

We created our own invitations and programs with a laptop and printer. Together we planned the entire wedding. We had no money, but what we did have was faith that God would bless us with the wedding of our dreams. Being that Tony was off work from a worsening spinal injury, his finances were not good. Nevertheless, we continued to plan. You may ask how we planned for a wedding with no money. I guess that question can be asked about all of the triumphs we have seen in the Bible. Do you believe Him for what you are asking for? If yes, then He will do it for you too!

Nicole's Dress

I was at work on my break looking at different dresses online, but nothing really stood out. I saw a dress that I could work with. It wasn't anything special to it, but I knew that I could accessorize and glam it up with jewelry. I told Tony and we decided to visit the store so that I could try it on. We were so non-traditional. I didn't care if he saw the dress or not... that was just us. In that short amount of time he became my best friend and I wanted to do everything with him; so we went!

They put me with a nice woman who was very helpful. She asked for the item number and shortly returned with the dress. I tried it on and I didn't like it at all. It did nothing for my shape and accessorizing would not have mattered. I needed something that would make him go WOW! So I looked for another dress. I looked and searched and I saw nothing, so I told Tony that we could leave and try some other places. As we were walking towards the door he spotted a dress hanging up and said, "What about this one?" I looked at the dress through the plastic and thought to myself, "Now if this dress is as beautiful on me as it is on the hanger, then this is it!"

I asked if I could see the dress, after the sales associate made sure nobody left it there to try on or buy, I was told I could try it on. The woman helping me brought me a veil, accessories and shoes to finish the look. When I came out Tony's eyes lit up! He said, "YES! This is the dress." I mean the dress was beautiful! It was just what I wanted! I needed no alterations other than a bustle to lift up the trail at the reception; so I wouldn't have to worry about the dress dragging. I heard people whispering about the dress as I walked back and forth in front of the mirrors and I thought to myself, "Someone is going to try and grab this dress."

I changed back into my clothes. I asked the woman who was helping me if the dress was the only one in the store. After checking she said that it was not only the last one in that size, but the only dress like it in the entire store. She said that if I purchased it in the store I would be able to put money down and make payments (like a layaway plan). However, if someone purchased it I would have to order it online, pay the balance in its entirety and have it shipped to the store. I told her that I understood and needed a second to think. She agreed to give me some time and went to help someone else. I had the dress lying across my forearm. I closed my eyes and said a prayer. I asked the Lord to hold the dress until I could purchase it. At that moment it fell in my spirit that someone was going to pay for my dress in its entirety. So by faith I marked my dress off the list of things to pay for. Next, we needed someone to do our flower arrangements and help to decorate the church.

A Planner!

A few weeks later my bridal party and I went to the place where I was going to purchase my dress. They needed to try on their dresses so that they could get the necessary alterations. As soon as I walked in the door I gave the person helping us the item number to the dress so that I could try it on. Glory be to God, the dress was still there! I tried on the dress and my bridesmaids loved it. This time there were more people there and admiring the dress. I even heard someone tell one of the brides that she needed to try the dress on after I took it off, but I was not worried. I was trusting God. I took the dress off and headed to the door as we were finished for the day.

On my way out of the door, I was stopped by a woman whom I had never met before. She said, "I gave my card to one of your bridesmaids. I do decorations, flower arrangements, bouquets and more for weddings. I was led to come to you and tell you that God told me to help you." I was in total shock! All I could say was, "Thank You Jesus!" This woman did not know our situation but God did! I was so excited and couldn't wait to get to the car so I could call Tony and tell him what had taken place. I knew it would blow his mind like it blew mine!

Weeks went by and Tony said to call the woman that approached me at the bridal store. I begin to go back and forth in my mind with thoughts like we don't have the money to pay her Lord. But I said, "We trust you God. You have set the date and "You" will make provision!" I called and she began to ask questions. She asked what our colors were along with a couple other questions and I told her. By the end of the conversation, we decided that we would meet at her house that weekend. When we got to her home she made us feel so comfortable. She told us that she was a minister of the gospel and how God began to speak to her when she saw me. She then led us into the basement where she creates. She already had my bouquet made with our colors as well as a box beautifully decorated for cards.

I was in shock! I was saying within myself, "Lord, I trust you for the money for all of this." Just then she said again, "God told me to help you. I get everything wholesale. Just give me $100 to get some things I need, I will take care of everything else you need me to do. She then said, "Pay me whatever you can." Tony and I began to praise God right in this woman's house! This was our first time ever meeting her. We didn't know her nor did she know us, but God divinely connected us! In one day our flower arrangements, my bouquet, the bridesmaids' flowers, boutonnieres that the groomsmen wear on the lapel of their jacket, my tiara (which she also purchased) and all the decorations for the church were taken care of! Not only that, Tony got a call from his Dad saying he wanted to give him $150. With that money we were able to hold the dress which was still at the store! Not only was the dress still there, it had gone on sale and $400 was knocked off the price! It was then that I knew for sure my dress was going to be paid for. In fact, Tony said as he was giving the cashier the money, "Somebody is going to pay for your dress". I told him the same had fallen in my spirit!

The Ring

We praised God as we saw everything coming together! Tony finally proposed to me. We were at his home sitting in the living room. We were working on some wedding plans and I stopped and said, "You know you never proposed?" I laughed. We got confirmation and just began planning. He then said, "I was waiting for the right time." I thought maybe it had something to do with him not being able to purchase a ring he desired for me at the time. He then pulled out a box and said, "You won't believe this but my mother found a ring and she gave it to me." He said the words I longed to hear. "Nicole, will you marry me?" His hand was shaking, he said he was playing...I don't think he was playing though. The ring was gold with a few diamonds, it was beautiful and it fit me to a T. It wasn't what he would have liked, but nonetheless there was a ring on my finger.

Some weeks later Tony asked me to come over to visit him after I got off of work because he had something for me. I was excited to see what he was talking about. I mean God was just on a roll with blessing us, so daily I waited with expectation to see just what He would do next. I got to the house and he showed me a black box. I was like, "ARE YOU SERIOUS?!!!!" He said, "Before I show you this, I want you to know that this was given to me!" "Given to you?!" I asked.

He said, "Yes. One of the sisters at the church was engaged, but it is no longer taking place. She asked if I had a ring to give you. First, I want you to know . . ." I stopped him and said, "I know the situation. I know if you had it you'd buy it and I am not marrying you for a ring. I know that God is in this and that's all I care about!" He smiled and opened the box. The ring was beautiful! The ring I had on was gold, but I wanted a white gold ring. It was perfect! I cried and I lifted my hands! I really wondered what did I do to deserve this?! It then fell in my spirit, "It is not that you deserve anything, but that you were obedient." I then said, "Thank you Lord Jesus!"

He Did It!

I was calling family members to get their address in order to send out the invitations. I called my aunt Toni who lived in Germany, but had returned to Maryland. She went on to say that the family really couldn't help much because of the recession. I told her, "The recession is the recession but I don't live by it, nor am I bound by it. I trust God! That's why I haven't had to ask anyone for a thing." She said, "Well, Alright! My wedding gift to you is your dress." I almost threw the phone up against the wall! When I told her I had one on hold, she asked how much and I told her the price. She told me I could come the following day to pick up the money and that it would be cash. I got off the phone and I began to cry and thank God!

Later I received another call that blew my mind. My father's friend Roger wanted to speak with me. When I called him he went on to say that he was taking classes and had a very expensive camera. He described it and all its features. I still did not know what he was talking about as I did not own a professional camera, but I was excited for him. Just then he said, "I am saying all of this because I want to take all of your pictures for your wedding as a gift to you and your future husband." He said, "My wife will make you all a personal photo album. I will be at your house the day of the wedding to take pictures of you while you are getting ready as well as at the church and the reception."

I began to cry and thank him! We did not know how we were going to pay to have pictures taken, but God had already "taken" care of that as well! On top of that Tony was given a huge deal on a Lincoln Navigator Limousine to pick up my bridal party and I from the house on the day of the wedding. I began to think about all we had gone through! I was told that our marriage would never be blessed and more, but God was truly showing me that His word is true! Romans 8:31, "What shall we then say to these things? If God be for us, who can be against us?" I was at work talking to my friend Peggy, who was my supervisor. I was telling her that God did what He promised. She then asked me did I have the money for a bustle. I told her I was trusting God. She pulled $50 from her purse and said, "Here is your wedding gift from me!" It was the exact amount I needed!

It's the Little Things!

I would just sit and think to myself, God you are so amazing! I messed up and fell so many times. I didn't allow that to stop me from staying with you and you blessed me! The lonely nights, the season of isolation, declining dates with potential prospects and outings with friends to seek your face was all worth it! I knew that marriage was not the end of my story, but just the beginning! I was so excited because although Tony and I had not known each other long, my dad was in agreement as well and was going to walk me down the aisle! I continued praying that God would make provision for all we needed. We had a list of things we had to purchase. One of the things I wanted was my favorite perfume, but it wasn't in the budget. I didn't have time to stress over the little things. God had provided greatly for us!

Tony and I didn't worry or stress at all! We did the invitations ourselves because it wasn't in the budget to have them done professionally. Although we didn't have the reception

136

hall at the time, we were going forward by faith. We didn't share this with anyone. We just enjoyed each other and continued to plan knowing that God would work things out. The sisters at my new church welcomed me in! One of my bridesmaids threw me a bridal shower at her house. I also got a call from another one of my bridesmaids saying she wanted to throw me a bachelorette party. You may say to yourself, o.k. Nicole, why is that such a big deal? The majority of the young women in my bridal party I had just met, so the love I was shown brought tears to my eyes.

One of the young ladies called and asked for my size, my favorite perfume and if there were other things I wanted or needed. I was so amazed! That was one of the things I desired, but wasn't able to get! I was later given specific instructions that included following one of them to D.C. I went into this nice restaurant and discovered that they had everything set up for me! They paid for my food and dessert which was not cheap! They had more gifts than I expected! I received a lot of nice under garments and oils as well. They had me feeling like Esther! At the end of the night I was dropped off at my car. As I drove home (now I could call it my home) I began thanking God that He provided not only what I needed, but even the little things I desired! Needless to say, it was a great night!

Tony stayed at one of his best friend's house so that I could stay at his house. I was so excited about that! That was my last night alone. After the wedding I no longer had to leave. I could stay the night and sleep in the same bed with my husband!

Those Who Wait On GOD

Chapter #24

The Day Has Finally Come

Tony's Version

The morning of the wedding was finally here. I was at my best man's house and felt quite refreshed because as a Man of God, a traditional bachelor's party was not for me. So, we spent the evening at Glory Days Restaurant, which was cool because I could invite the Lord. Call me corny, but I was delivered and wanted to stay that way. Above all, I loved God more than a stripper or a good time. I was not nervous, I was ready! I knew without a shadow of a doubt that this is the one God had for me before the foundation of the world.

I was in my bishop's office waiting for the word to go into the sanctuary. While waiting, my groomsmen and I took pictures. The wedding was supposed to start at noon. Around 12:10 pm I still had not gotten the word to come out, so I sent word that we were going to start; it didn't matter who wasn't there. I had in my mind that this wedding was not for everybody else, but for me and my bride to be. My bishop was in place so I was ready to roll.

I remember the sanctuary doors opening and there she was... just beautiful. When she got close enough for me to see her face we both laughed. The wedding was literally 40 minutes and it was over. We headed from the church over to the place where we were holding the reception, which was paid in full the same week! We had fun with family and friends. But the most memorable moment was us leaving the reception and going straight to the airport for our flight to Rome, Italy. Our prayer was to leave our reception and go directly to our honeymoon and we did. It was one of the most blessed feelings that I have ever felt in my life.

Nicole's Version

On February 21, 2009 I woke up early in the morning. Tony was staying at his best man's house and I stayed at his house. I stood there in the bathroom looking in the mirror. I began thinking back to when God spoke to me and said I was no one's girlfriend, but someone's wife. Now I am looking in the mirror and I was about to be Mrs. Nicole Hinton. The tears began to fall as I thanked God. It was so surreal. The day had finally come and everything was in place. We were not only able to book our reception at a very nice place, but we were also able to fly out to Rome, Italy immediately after the reception, just like I prayed.

I turned around and looked into the hall where my dress was hanging on the door. I wasn't going to have to return this one! It was all so special. It was like a wedding gift from God. I wasn't nervous, I wasn't anxious; I was in awe of God! I took that moment to pray before the makeup artist got there. After prayer I received a text from Tony saying he loved me and he'd see me at the altar.

Now at the altar…my dad grabs my arm and asks, "Are you ready to do this?" I was thinking to myself, "Really daddy?" But I knew he was just being a dad. I replied, "Yes! I am so ready!" He said, "Okay. I love you and I am happy for you." He gave me a hug and we went through the doors. As I went down the aisle it was like I had tunnel vision. I didn't notice who was on either side of me.

All I noticed was my handsome groom. Everything I went through, every counterfeit, every set back, my disobedience, my running and my partying; now here I was on this day saved and going into a marriage that was ordained by God! It was the happiest day of my life! After I kissed my groom and we walked down that aisle I knew that it was not only a walk to a natural destination, but to a spiritual one. I went down that aisle a wife, soon to be a mom and ready to birth out purpose!

Coming Home

After a week spent in Italy, it felt good coming to "our" home and being able to enjoy the benefits of marriage. God's way felt good! We took two whole weeks to enjoy ourselves. The second week we spent time staying up late reading the heartfelt cards people sent. We opened our gifts and talked all night long. Nicole and I looked at some furniture some time ago and there was a really nice bedroom set that we liked and really wanted. One of my desires was not to put my wife in the bed that I had since I was 18. It was defiled, if you know what I mean; so we were sleeping on a blow up bed.

Guess what? God did it again! After reading all the cards from the wedding, the monetary gifts equaled the exact amount needed for our new bedroom set. God is faithful, He honors when you do it His way! It was imperative that we took the time to develop our relationship with God in our season of singleness because had we not, the storms that we were to face would have wiped us out. After the Honeymoon was over, real life began...

Those Who Wait On GOD
Word Of Encouragement From The Authors

Tony's Word of Encouragement

If I had one word to express to the readers of this book it would be "WAIT!" I do not care if you have been waiting for years for a spouse. Do not believe that the Lord has forgotten you. Again, He has not forgotten you! Every prayer you have prayed will come to pass. Women, be graceful during the wait. Don't be desperate, men do not like a desperate female who is willing to "give the milk for free". Let that sink in. If you appear desperate then you become prey for the enemy. He will send every man that is the complete opposite of the one God wants you to be with. On the outside he may look right, but on the inside, his motives are wrong. Judas looked just like the rest of the disciples, but he had another agenda! Many women have entered relationships because they feel that they have been waiting too long and because this man popped up, it has to be God. Do not be deceived. Wait!

Men, while you wait for your wife prepare a place for her. Ensure you have something to bring to the table. You cannot ask God for a spouse and you are not in the position to provide a stable living environment. Do not prepare for just the tangible things but spiritual strength and fortification. Can you pray, NO... can you pray and get results? Do you hear from God and obey His voice when He speaks? As the head we have to be in position at all times; spiritually, mentally and physically. Pick a day to fast and stay consistent.

Do you know what your calling is? If not why are you asking for a help meet? What is she going to help you to do if you don't know what you are to do yourself? As the man, seek God for your spouse. Just because we have the "upper hand" and we "findeth" our wives does not mean this decision is up to us. Man of God, pray and seek the Lord and prepare a plan for your new family now. What areas are you interested in living? What school district do you want your children to attend? What things will you pursue now to prepare for your new family? We are saved, but we have to be practical. Overall, keep God first and He will add everything else that you need and desire.

If you were once married and you know you entered the marriage out of disobedience (or even in obedience, but the person just left you) and the marriage ended- trust God. He is the God of the second chance, it's not over. I believe you will have a chance for love again, but you have to remember the first mistake and avoid it this time around. Pray, believe and watch God work. Get excited! Although I was not married before, He has forgiven me after all that I have done and been through. Surely you are not exempt. Be blessed.

Nicole's Word of Encouragement

I would have never imagined that I would be married, let alone living for God! In my season of singleness I found that I could live without a man, but I could not live without God. God knows the motives of our hearts. Practicing purity or abstaining from sex does not make your process any shorter or any longer. We don't enter into the wait with any other motive but to please God. We are presenting our bodies as a living sacrifice because Jesus paid the ultimate price! No man took His life, but He willingly laid it down so that we can have everlasting life. We don't endure all we do just to get a man and start a family. At the end of the day the ultimate goal in the life of a Christian is not marriage, but heaven.

It is imperative to seek God as a single woman. Everything you need now (while single) will prepare you for marriage. If you don't pray now marriage will not make you pray. If you aren't practicing abstinence now then you will find it difficult to abstain or resist temptation within your marriage. If you aren't fasting now marriage will not make you ...wait maybe it will! I laughed at that too, but seriously, what I am saying is that this has to be a lifestyle!

You need to know how to be kept in your singleness and as a wife. When you are married you do not go blind and it does not mean that temptation stops. We must first learn how to be faithful to God without the man so He can trust us with the man. We must not make a spouse an idol before he comes. Some of you are asking, "How can I do that if he isn't physically here Nicole?" Well one of the signs that you are at risk of or have made him an idol is if you get angry at God for not sending him and every year he (the husband) doesn't come you draw further away from God.

Another sign is you don't spend much time in prayer, but when you do your only focus is asking for a husband. Now don't think that it is wrong to desire a husband. You aren't desperate because you ask God to send and/or reveal to you your spouse. As I said early on, I prayed for my husband and asked God to reveal things to me concerning him, but at the end of the day, I understood that there were more things that I needed to be concerned about like my Kingdom Assignment. I still needed to know what God was doing in and through me. I needed to know what my weapons were, (meaning my spiritual gifts) and how to operate in them and be effective.

Some of you have lost focus because you feel that God is taking too long. You have thought about making "the process" go a little faster than it has been going. You are thinking about how you can become a mommy now just in case God doesn't do it for you. There are many reasons that the husband has not come yet and it has nothing to do with being a good Christian. If that were the case none of us would have spouses. It would have ceased after sin entered the Garden of Eden. The word of God tells us that no good thing dwells in our flesh. God does not punish his children by not giving them a spouse. God is not petty! There can be numerous reasons why he has not come. Maybe you need to deepen your relationship with God; He wants more time with you because of where He is taking you. Maybe your children have to be born in a certain time and season in which God will use them mightily!

As a single woman it is good that you stay busy and stay focused. Stay focused on your God given assignment. You are worth the wait. You have read my testimony and still this is only a portion. There is no way it can all fit inside this book, but I will tell you that you do not have to settle for a counterfeit. You don't have to settle because you have a child by him or because you live with him! You may have been told that you will never find someone to love you or accept you and your children. You may feel like you have too much baggage, you have too many scars, you have gone too far or that your past is too messy, but there is NOTHING too hard for God!

If He did it for me than He can do that and more for you! My mess, my hurt, my embarrassment and shame has turned into a book that is glorifying God because He

144

brought me out! Right where you are sitting, standing at the bus stop, riding the train, flying on the plane, in church or class when you should be paying attention or lying beside the man you know God is telling you is not the one He has chosen- make the decision that today you are going to LIVE! You are going to live for God and do it HIS way! You would be surprised how faith and works are intertwined. It's not about your biological clock ticking. He knows your clock better than you do! He knows how old you are and how long you have been waiting; will you trust him? I pray you are encouraged through our testimony and if you haven't already, I pray that you will decide to stay with God and be one who will wait on Him, not only for a spouse, but to see who He has truly called you to be!

Conclusion

When God gives us a glimpse of what He has promised, we rarely consider all it will take to receive it. Just when you think you have been dealt a difficult hand in life as an adult or in your childhood, you begin to realize that as you walk with God, He can use it all. God was and is preparing you by allowing situations in life to strategically position you at the opportune time and season to come in contact with your destiny. What God is preparing you for is Greater than you can imagine.

Acknowledgements & Special Thanks!

First and foremost we give honor and glory to God. In the process of us putting this book together we realized how true the gift of writing is for us. There would be no book if God had not given us the testimony. We would not have had the confidence to go forth in writing this if it were not for the faith we have in our Lord and Savior Jesus Christ. You receive all the glory!

We also want to give a special thanks to our Bishop Jerome Stokes, Lady Marsha Stokes, LaTonya Gibson , Apostle Donine Wallace, Apostle Winston Wallace Jr., Apostle Chris Christian, Evangelist Sharon Booker, Courtney Goff, Maree Gaines, Robin Kindrick, LaTreya Edwards, Dana Kirby, Sinead Warner, Amber Thomas, Angel Wilder, Anthony Wilder, Laura Spencer, Shakita Ellerbe, Monica Hampton, Shawanda Taylor, Lakeisha Bethea, Rhonda Starling, Yetta Eagleman, Melanie Yellowday, Chalita Walden, Kee Frazier, Lisa Gordon, Shannon Peterson, Christina Litiskas, Shanese Campbell, Fa'tima Carmichael, La'Tivia Elizabeth, Francine Ott, Maja Kolonja, Nahkeekah Wall, Nicole Flores, Shanika Miles, Azalea Salter, Faneisha Ragin, Stacie Dickson, Vanita Welch, Tiara Codwell, Sharon Young, Anita Nyambuza, Patricia Joseph, Dawn Yerger, Joyce Hargrove, Peggy Downs, Menuch I, Quinisha White and Jennell Dixon for their support and contributions towards helping us publish our book. Special thanks to La'Tivia Elizabeth Tipton for editing our book!

Contact Information:

Email us:
tnhintonspeaks@yahoo.com

Like us on Facebook:
https://www.facebook.com/ThoseWhoWaitOnGod

Follow us on our Instagram:
@thosewhowaitongod

Subscribe to Nicole's Channel on YouTube:
https://www.youtube.com/user/iambcuzofu

Made in the USA
Charleston, SC
24 March 2016